What others are saying...

"In our Western hemisphere where denial or suppression of sadness, pain and illness is often the norm, Ulrike Hobbs-Scharner expands our awareness through details which illustrate that the natural phenomenon of death, experienced by so many as a tragedy, is only transformation into a world of higher order."
— Gerhard Schmidt, Author and Teacher

"*Dancing on the Other Side* is one of the most important comprehensive books written on the taboo topic of death. After my mother passed away this extraordinary book confirmed and taught me to understand some of the visions I myself experienced. Finally a book that actually educates you and helps to accept the mystery of death."
— Beate & Matthias Weber, Emmy-winning composer, songwriter, music editor (Pearl Harbor, TV Sopranos, The Shield and West Wing)

"Throughout the lives of many people death is the big unknown and a fearful event in Christian mythology. Ulrike Hobbs-Scharner's knowledge and wisdom take away sinister foreboding and reveal death as a natural part of life. At last a book that gives answers, guidance and comfort to the daunting questions surrounding death. An ideal complement to the Tibetan Book of the Dead."
— Christian v. Bodecker & Dr. Horst Schöll, M.D.

"This book is a rare jewel that opened an entirely new path to me towards understanding death. Since reading it, my attitude towards death and dying has relaxed greatly."

— Monika Borchers

"The dialogues with the dead in the spiritual world move me again and again. These reports convey such warmth and love that they chase away fears of death, that great mystery. Transition to the non-physical dimension of being appears so natural, so close..."

— Ursula Reinhardt, Ph.D. Art & Art History

Dancing
on the
Other Side
beyond death

Ulrike Hobbs-Scharner

Translated from the German
by Heidi Knott
and Clio Osman

Dancing on the Other Side: Beyond Death
Copyright © 2011 by Ulrike Hobbs-Scharner
Translated by Heidi Knott

All rights reserved. No portion of this book may be reproduced in whole or in part, by any means whatever, except for passages excerpted for purposes of review, without the prior written permission of the publisher. For information, or to order additional copies, please contact:

RoseLight Publishng
PO Box 589
Philo, CA 95466
roselightpublishing@gmail.com

Cover and book design by Mike Brechner / Cypress House
Cover graphic by Martel DuVigneaud
Diagrams by Daglef Seeger, Freiburg, Germany

Publisher's Cataloging-In-Publication Data

Hobbs-Scharner, Ulrike.
  [Der Tod: ein grosses Geheimnis (English)]
  Dancing on the other side : beyond death / Ulrike Hobbs-Scharner ; translated from the German by Heidi Knott. -- 1st ed. -- Philo, CA: RoseLight Pub., c2011.
  p. ; cm.
  ISBN: 978-0-9832856-0-1
  Originally published as: Der Tod : ein grosses Geheimnis? (Vörstetten : HMHE-Verl., 2007).
   Includes bibliographical references.
   1. Future life. 2. Death--Psychological aspects. 3. Thanatology. 4. Spiritualism. 5. Mind and body. 6. Self-actualization (Psychology) 7. Spirituality. 8. Life after death. I. Knott, Heidi, 1949- II. Title.
BL535 .H6313 2011   2011920801
133.901/3--dc22 2011

Printed in Canada

2 4 6 8 9 7 5 3 1

First edition

*Before there was a garden, vines or grapes
In this world,
We were already drunk
With the wine of eternal life.*
　　　　— Jalal ad-Din Rumi

Contents

Preface xi
One: Is It True That No One Has Ever Come Back? 1
Two: Death Always Comes Too Soon 11
Three: Dying Naturally Through Old Age 17
Four: Prolonged or Sudden Death Due to Severe Illness ... 27
Five: Caring for the Dying 29
Six: Death from the Perspective of Those Left Behind 39
Seven: Death from the Perspective of the Deceased 43
Eight: How Souls Make Contact With Those Still on Earth .. 47
Nine: Help Through Soul Guides and Relatives
Who Have Already Crossed the Threshold 61
Ten: The Transition Zone 67
Eleven: Coming Home 81
Twelve: The Astral World 87
Thirteen: The Death of a Child 95
Fourteen: The Wake 101

Fifteen: The Schooling Centers 111
Sixteen: Soul Guides and Angels 123
Seventeen: The Bewildered Soul 131
Eighteen: Violent Death 139
Nineteen: Help for Souls Who Are Grounded 147
Twenty: Life's Calling 151
Twenty-one: The Council of The Wise Ones 155
Twenty-two: The Soul Self and the Ego Self 167
Twenty-three: Raising the Energy Frequency 175
Twenty-four: Prayers for the Dying 179

    General Prayers 182
    Prayers at the Bedside of the Dying 185
    For the Very Ill 193
    For Coma Patients 194
    For Those Who Died Early 196
    For Those Who Have Just Died 197
    In Cases of Suicide 198
    At the Gravesite 200
    Prayers for Blessing and Protection 202

Notes and Bibliography 207

Dancing
on the
Other Side

Preface

In late 2004, the tsunami in Southeast Asia took hundreds of thousands of lives, and was followed by a wave of horror and compassion throughout the world. An unimaginable number of people died. Thousands more were plunged into misery and hardship, desperately seeking their relatives, without even a bare minimum to sustain themselves. The world's ability to help was concentrated on this enormous suffering.

In the weeks that followed, I assisted many people in a world not visible to our physical eyes. I helped the deceased make the transition into the purely spiritual world. In the first chapter I will describe how I am able to do such work.

It is almost impossible to relate how appalled I was that untold numbers of people who had lost their lives through this catastrophe had become completely confused and disorientated, and had no way of conceiving that they were no longer on the earthly plane, that they no longer had physical bodies. To be dead and in this condition is a living nightmare. It struck me that a surprising number of these dead, who were unable to understand their own physical deaths, came from Western countries.

After the first shock, it once again became clear to me that in our culture, dealing with the subject of death is still in its infancy. Death is a subject that is either taboo or surrounded by fear. Even though death is inevitable, we neglect spiritual confrontation with it. If at all, most of us concern ourselves only superficially with issues that pertain to death. What a loss! For here, dear reader, lies a sublime and unfathomable treasure waiting to be discovered.

In my unusual work, I have repeatedly experienced that, for many who have died, it has been nearly impossible for them to recognize their own transformation if they hadn't already addressed the theme of life after death while alive on Earth. Those, however, who widen their consciousness in regard to the existence of life after death, or who develop a deep religious faith before they die, will more easily find their way in the changed circumstances after their deaths.

Since my experience with the tsunami, I have decided to venture out and talk about my many years of experience as an out-of-body visitor to other dimensions. I want to show that life never ends — it continues in other spheres and in different forms. Great uplifting forces are behind this. They are so surprisingly different from our way of thinking that we must make some fundamental changes. Allow yourself a fascinating look into a different sphere of being.

Ulrike Hobbs-Scharner
2011

One

Is It True That No One Has Ever Come Back?

We live in the 21st century, and on our planet Earth practically every region has been explored. Our highly developed satellite system allows us to reach anyone anywhere via cell phones or landlines, radio or television, not to mention the Internet. But what about when someone we love dies? Is the connection then broken? For most of us, it is unsettling to discover that we really don't know.

The world that we believe we know is the material, visible, measurable, and researchable universe. It consists of clearly defined objects, is three-dimensional, and can be perceived with our five senses. Our planet's physical world is a familiar plane of existence, which we can understand even though some things seem quite remarkable. On the other hand, planes of being that extend beyond the three-dimensional world may be theoretically calculable. Scientists postulate planes of being that they call the eight-dimensional hyperspace of Minkowski. Yet nothing is known about how we as individual souls feel or live there, how we as soul-consciousness observe and interpret there, or how infinite and all-inclusive we are. We walk through life blindly, confident that we are seeing everything.

This book is based on hundreds of diary notations that I made upon returning from my many out-of-body experiences. From this vast resource, I have chosen the experiences that relate to the fourth dimension, a plane where the eternal expression of the soul is no longer under the influence of the individual genetic makeup or limited by the chemical processes of the physical body. I wish to state explicitly that nothing in this book has been fabricated, that no experience has been altered or embellished. The narratives are very personal ones that someone else with similar capacities might describe in a slightly different way. While we are all individuals and see the world in unique ways through the eyes of our own consciousness, that in no way changes the events and content of the narratives that follow. There is no death, for life never ends!

When I was ten years old, I had an appendectomy. I still distinctly remember all the preparations prior to being anesthetized. Very shortly after that, I saw myself hovering above the operating table and I heard the assistants joke that this was my doctor's first operation. Then I was rolled to the recovery room where I continued to hover above my body, listening to the attending nurses' conversation. Suddenly I felt a gentle tug, and I realized I was in my body again and opened my eyes. Afterward, when I related these events and my impressions to the nurses, none of them believed me. I decided then that I would not tell anyone else about it. Years passed, and though I still remembered the event as clearly as when it had happened, I didn't contemplate the subject at all. Later, out of a deep spiritual need, I began to intensively pursue spiritual questions and meditation techniques. As time went on, I had the privilege of meeting some unusual people, in Asia and Europe, who became my teachers on my path of spiritual development. I have much to thank them for.

About twenty years after the appendectomy, I was on holiday with my family. We were staying in a small cabin on an island in the middle of a beautiful lake. There once again I had an out-of-body experience. My husband and the children were away shopping. I remained on "our" island and lay down on the bed to rest. After a while I felt my body totally relax and a strange numbness or immobility gradually overcome me. It intensified to the point where I couldn't move a single limb. Then I felt a slight but growing trembling go through my body, accompanied by a high ringing tone — whether it was within or outside of it I couldn't say. Unable to move my head, arms, or legs, I was awake and fully conscious. Lying on my back, I was in no way distressed by the loudness of the unusual ringing. Then, all at once I felt a part of myself rolling out of my physical body. Yes, "rolling out" is how I would describe it. In a split second I was standing upright in the room, looking at my physical body as if it were an object. Only then did I become aware of the overwhelming reality — *I am not my outer shell; that is still lying there. What I really am is standing beside it, observing it.* A thought that coursed through me, overwhelming me was, *Oh, my God, I am not my physical body!*

To my amazement, I felt as if I were in a compact, firm body. I could think, see my arms and legs, and even touch them with my hands. My arms and hands looked like dense clouds consisting of millions of yellow, white, and blue points of light. It is not easy to describe this experience in words, as the points of light were moving, but also still; they changed and yet remained constant and unchanging. My present form seemed identical to that which was lying on the bed. Then, without my doing, there was a strong tug in the direction of my physical body, like the one I had experienced at the time of my appendectomy, and for a moment I felt the previous numbness, which quickly vanished. I sprang from the bed full of enthusiasm, and ran wildly around the room shouting, "Now I know that I'm immortal!" My entire being was flooded with endless joy and thankfulness. I knew with deep certainty that my soul was only temporarily housed in my physical body. Of course, I was filled with questions, but deep inside I was also sure that I would find all the answers.

In the weeks that followed, my original excitement and enthusiasm calmed down. I wished to repeat my experience, but it rarely happened. The more I reflected on what had taken place, the more I realized how profoundly something within me had changed. I was very keen to learn more, but at the time there was very little information available about out-of-body experiences. The books *Return From Tomorrow* [1] and *I Was Clinically Dead* [2] helped me only a little. When I spoke with friends or relatives about it, I was met mostly with misunderstanding and skepticism, so I got used to talking as little as possible about my experiences and instead wrote about them in my diary. Also, I made a habit of lying down once a day and carefully observing my body as it relaxed completely and then became immobile and heavier until the high ringing tone would begin. The biggest problem was to remain wide-awake. If I was too tired, I would fall asleep. If I was too active, my body couldn't come to rest. It was important to find the right moment and to raise my consciousness above the familiar patterns of thought. I had to stay awake and clear so that my attention was deflected away from my physical body, yet at the same time allow deepest relaxation, until I was finally able to roll out or float above. In the beginning, there were many instances that I couldn't understand or find a context for: suddenly, I would clearly hear my name being called or I would feel unusual waves of vibrations moving through my body. Also, I heard various humming tones and sounds that always brought my consciousness back to my body. With that the exercise failed. Only when I became more relaxed and realized that all these phenomena were integral to the exercise did I find it increasingly easy to practice.

In the years that followed, my ability to leave my physical body matured. The exercises became more and more effective, and I was able to leave the body more quickly. I gained a new understanding about the nonphysical world and its energetic principles. In the beginning, I was always accompanied by a spiritual teacher so that I could increasingly experience the wonders of out-of-body existence. I was often overwhelmed by the intensity of the light, by the ability to communicate without words, by the fascinating and multifaceted beings whom I encountered there, and by their incredible beauty. Everywhere, timelessness whispered to me, "Love is the beginning of all things, love is the key."

I learned that I could break through barriers and experience other dimensions only by concentrating my energy on the divine. To truly direct my energy, I had first to become quiet and still. I could only be in spheres that corresponded to my own inner light. Every soul lives in a certain soul-frequency that is determined by one's own individual development. How much one can appreciate the wonders of the divine depends on one's level of consciousness. The highest and purest frequency of love is so intense and so immeasurably powerful that one can only retreat from the blinding intensity of light, or slowly adjust to this frequency through inner spiritual growth. If one does live in God's Light, then continual growth and healing ensue.

We are all multidimensional beings, though on Earth we mainly focus our consciousness on and identify with material things. Today, however, there are more and more reports and books describing near-death experiences and knowledge gained through out-of-body experiences, as well as from waking dreams (in which one dreams that one is dreaming). Everyone who has had such an experience agrees that his or her life has been profoundly changed. I personally experience the miracle of being liberated from heavy matter as a special gift. The ability to exist outside my physical limits has vastly expanded my awareness. The often-heard opinion that "no one has ever come back" is wrong and merely a sign of the one-sided ability of those expressing such sentiments. I wish to make it very clear that I am most certainly not the only one who is able to go back and forth between the material and spiritual worlds. All over the world there are many human beings with this ability — either because they have learned the necessary technique or because they "brought the capacity with them."[3]

Terms such as "development" and "progress" must no longer be applied exclusively to technology, physics, or medicine. They also refer to flexibility and expansion of consciousness, where consciousness can recognize and rediscover itself in all levels of space and energy in the multidimensional universe. Unfortunately, this is often dismissed in our modern scientific world, which primarily recognizes what we can see, hear, smell, feel, and taste, or that which can be determined through testing and reproduction according to scientific criteria. The rich and real treasures that are gained through subjective, individual experiences and inner spiritual evolution are almost always categorically denied. Whether consciously or unconsciously, Westerners in particular, with their one-sided materialistic and rationalistic view of life, have put a narrow framework around the scope of their knowledge by accepting only scientific methodology as the criterion for absolute truth. For lack of alternatives, or perhaps for fear of straying from familiar terrain, they often vehemently defend their viewpoint. Other paths toward knowledge are ridiculed or dismissed as preposterous.

The more we humans are able to shed our fear of inner evolution and awareness the stronger "the divine fire of eternal love" can shine within us.[4] This fire alone can lead us beyond all boundaries of time and space.

For a long time I had a spiritual master who helped me understand the nonphysical world. Later I was given the task of helping other souls. In the many dialogues that follow, where the word "Guide" is used, I am referring to myself. This is also the case with all the quotations from my diaries. I would like to add that in talking about the nonmaterial world in this book, I share my views as a Christian. In the broadest sense, however, these narratives of the spiritual world are just as valid for people of all religions, as well as for atheists. The divine does not depend upon any form of belief or upon whether we believe at all.

May this book and the selected dialogues it contains communicate some insights into the state of being after our physical death. I would also ask you to keep in mind that all the pictures and ideas are relative and are limited by the meager words available to describe the complex spiritual world. We all have differing concepts of the other side. Every religion has created its own "heaven." Behind them all is the Eternal One, this Creative Power that we call "God," tirelessly moving us to seek that which has no boundaries. So while the chapters in this book have their limitations and afford only a tiny glimpse of immeasurable infinity, perhaps, step by step, they can bring us closer to it.

Two

Death Always Comes Too Soon

For many of us it is disconcerting and sometimes even frightening to think about death and dying, because we are confronted with a total mystery. It's like taking a trip to a distant, foreign land without knowing what to expect. It takes courage to embark on a journey into the unknown, to prepare for an adventure. In our day-to-day lives we usually feel safe because our surrounding environment is full of trusted, familiar things. We have contact with people we love. Friends and neighbors are close by, as are animals, trees, and plants that we know. No wonder, then, that death seems to be an enemy, because it tears us away from them all. Unhappily, so we think, death always comes too soon.

When the hour draws near in which we must (or may) leave our physical bodies, the process of dying has immense significance. It is extremely important that we begin this journey with calm and confidence — which is possible.

Reports from all epochs and all the world's regions describe how people have crossed the threshold into the next dimension in deep harmony and great peace.

Knowledge about the meaning of life does not come through intellectual learning alone. The great spiritual laws that govern the universe will only be revealed to those who are seekers, searching for the path of self-knowledge. One learns who one really is, and becomes watchful for messages and answers, which are often given in small ways.

There is countless evidence for life after death. Nonetheless, it usually does not form a part of our "collective" consciousness. A pioneering researcher on this subject was Dr. Raymond Moody, who collected numerous reports from people who had had near-death experiences. All of them had been clinically dead and were revived, after which they talked about their near-death experiences and of crossing over into a different dimension. Moody noted that while each and every one had had his own unique experience, still there were many elements in their stories that were similar or even the same. Those interviewed were aware that they had left their physical bodies. All had seen themselves as separated from the body while looking down on it. All of them were absolutely clear about what had happened.

One of Moody's patients related the following:

I thought, now I am dead, but not with regret. I simply couldn't figure out where I should be going next. My thinking and consciousness were exactly the same as when I was alive, but I was still unable to explain the present situation. I kept thinking, where should I be going? What should I do? And My God, I'm dead. I can't believe it!" This is because we never really think it is possible, never completely believe, that we will die. That is something that only happens to others. While we somehow know it, deep in our hearts we never really fully believe it.[5]

According to Moody, after dying, many people see their relatives or the doctor who is treating them. Frequently, the dead want to contact them, but are unsuccessful because those who are living in the material world cannot recognize them:

I watched as I was being revived. It was really very strange. I wasn't actually floating very high above. It was almost as though I were standing on a podium that wasn't much higher than the others. I was just able to see over their heads. I tried to talk to them, but no one could hear me. Nobody listened to me.

Again and again in the many reports of near-death experiences, people describe how they perceived their physical bodies from a different perspective. Often the dead are

Diagram 1

floating. For example, they experience themselves above the scene of the accident, over the bed, in the hospital, or at home.

> *I was above the scene of the accident and saw my seriously injured, lifeless body lying there. I saw the whole scene at one and the same time, clearly and transparently, from different positions. I also saw my car and the people who were standing around the accident. I watched as a small and strong fifty-five-year-old man tried to call me back to life. I heard exactly what all the observers were saying to each other. In fact, I could understand their thoughts. I heard the doctor say, 'I can't massage his heart—it's no use. There is nothing more to be done, he's dead.' I almost had to laugh at this, because I knew that I was alive, because I wasn't dead....[6]*

The dead person who finds himself in this unusual circumstance discovers that he has a second "body" that has a form just as his physical body does. He notices that his understanding and perception are much greater and much clearer than when he was "alive."

All of us will die eventually. We cannot escape death. It is as natural to die as it is to breathe. Death is not the end, but rather the beginning of a new life in a different dimension. When we die, there are four possible ways to leave our physical bodies:

- » dying slowly through natural aging;
- » a slow or quick death through a terminal disease;
- » dying because of an accident;
- » through murder or suicide.

Everyone who dies experiences death as a radiant, divine liberation from his or her physical organism with all its weaknesses and limitations of one kind or another. For someone who has a terminal illness and suffers agonizing pain, death comes as a great divine blessing. Death is also a blessing for accident victims. In every situation, death is the absolute deliverer from all physical pain, from conceptions, wishes, and visions of the future. "Conceptions" here refers to fixed ideas about character or personal circumstances, which are deeply subjective and have no real basis, such as "I am too fat or too thin, I am not handsome enough, I have no money, I can't do this or that." An abrupt end to life can also be disappointing, but the dead change their thinking very quickly, because each one finds help through his guardian angel and the many guides in the new dimension.

Three

Dying Naturally Through Old Age

The Process of Dying

What I am about to describe is what a person experiences through the natural aging process. The same thing happens when there is a long and difficult illness; it becomes very distorted, however, by pain and feeling unwell, and so it doesn't occur as gradually as when we age.

The transition, or passing over, from our earthly dimension into the next higher dimension is prepared for slowly, as one after the other the essential forces — earth, water, air, and fire — release themselves from the physical body. (In the Asian concept of the spiritual world, ether is also included.) These four elements relate to the characteristics of earth, water, air, and fire in the body. The body's liquids, blood, urine, saliva, lymph, etc., are considered the water element. Body warmth, which is needed for the digestive process, is the fire element. Breathing and circulation belong to the air element, and the bones are assigned to the earth element.

These diverse elements begin to dissipate during the dying process, which, in a healthy person, can take one to two years. As healthy people we can observe and experience this process, because it always shows the same signs:

The first element to "dissolve" is the heaviest, the earth element. It is absorbed into the next "finer" element, the subtle water element. An old person feels himself becoming heavier and heavier and moves only with great effort. His arms and legs stiffen and move more slowly. He is reluctant to walk and is content to sit at home. Movement is so limited that he feels as if he weighs a ton. Coordination and control over the body decrease steadily until they practically cease. A first sign that an older person is getting ready to make the transition into the next dimension is that he suddenly falls. He doesn't trip, but falls for no apparent reason at all. He also becomes increasingly tired.

The next stage is when the water element "dissolves" into the finer, more subtle element of fire. The outward sign is increasing loss of control over one's body fluids. Swallowing becomes strenuous because there is less saliva. The skin withers and loses elasticity, and wrinkles increase. It becomes harder to hold in one's urine. Digestion takes longer. In addition, an old person's memory begins to lapse more and more. Usually, long-term memory remains intact, but short-term memory weakens considerably, and he quickly forgets. One particular phenomenon begins to manifest itself in this second stage and persists until death: one often sees relatives who have already passed on. Parents, a spouse, or other close friends appear. Sometimes, though more rarely, angels or other beings of light are seen. Occasionally, I have heard younger people living in a house with older people say, "Grandma is going crazy, she isn't right in her head." This is really not the case at all; the old person's etheric covering has begun to withdraw, so that the next higher dimension is easier to experience.

Witness Report

"We met for a family festivity. We were all gathered around and, as it is when relatives get together, we spoke about many things, laughed, and ate together.

Grandfather and grandmother didn't say much at all, but they felt good in the family circle. Usually they got up earlier and went to bed long before the rest of us. But today grandfather suddenly got up and went to the living room cabinet, opened the door to the small bar, and brought out four glasses, filling each with whiskey. I asked him, 'Grandfather, what are you doing?' He answered, 'Don't you see that the hunters are coming, they are standing at the door.'

In earlier times grandfather always went hunting with his friends, and when they came back to his house, they always drank whiskey together. His hunting friends had all been dead for some years."

— Monika from Freiburg

In the third stage of dissolution, the fire element is absorbed by the next subtler element of air. Now the body begins to lose its warmth. The old person's feet and hands are cold to the tips. She needs a hot water bottle more frequently or an extra woolen blanket. The cold spreads until it finally reaches the heart. Food can't be digested properly, and eating becomes torturous. Some years ago I visited a family. Their grandmother was bedridden and often refused to eat. Her daughter scolded her: "You can't starve yourself to death here!" Not realizing that older people eat less and less, or that when they are dying, can refuse to eat at all, the daughter forced her mother to eat what she had prepared by spoon-feeding her. Shortly afterward her mother would throw it all up.

In the end, the element of air dissolves into ether, the element of space. At this stage, observers will notice that the older person breathes differently. Exhalations become longer and, at the same time, inhalations become shallower. Sometimes the dying exhale in long sighing breaths until, in the end, they stop breathing altogether.

Witness Report

"I promised Conrad that I would stay with his wife in the hospital where she lay dying. He couldn't be there himself as their daughter, Louise, was being confirmed on that day.

I was glad to sit by her bed. She could hardly speak anymore. Her skin was so pale and thin it seemed transparent. Her eyes were shut, and occasionally I would bend over carefully to hear whether she was still breathing.

Everything seemed so quiet and still. Her exhaling was shallow and long, I think about two minutes, and her inhaling was short, sometimes even accompanied by a sigh. Since I didn't know what to say, I decided to softly sing a song: "God has told his angels to watch over you, to protect you on your way." I sang this verse over and over again, probably for two or three hours.

Suddenly, Karin opened her eyes, looked at me with a wide-open and clear gaze, and died with a wonderful, fulfilled smile on her face. I felt myself so blessed and elated, for I felt the holy presence of many angels in the room. What a gift to be able to experience her passing over."

—Katinka from B.

The Etheric Body

A person observing the dying process might think that it is over, because "the threshold has been crossed" and the person is dead, but actually, at this point a very important internal process is going on that lasts for some time. Once the elements have dissolved completely into the ether, two polar energies begin to flow at one and the same time toward the heart: one from the pineal gland in the brain, and the other from the region of the coccyx (the bottom of the spine). This process is described precisely and fully in Tibetan Buddhism.[7] They say that Bindu essence (light essence) has begun to move. These two streams are also appropriately called Yin/Yang energy. This concentrated light essence is clearly observed by the consciousness of the dying person. White light flows from the pineal gland while orange-red light flows from the bottom vertebra into the center of the heart. Both essences circle around the etheric heart. Regardless of whether the dying person is a man or a woman, the process is always the same:

» From the pineal gland flows white light (yang energy) directly into the center of the heart.

» From the coccyx, or root chakra, flows the orange-red light (yin energy) also directly into the center of the heart.

> » As these two essences stream together and then circulate within the heart, they create for the dying a vision of a tunnel. He sees a passageway at the end of which there is often a white light or the beginning of a sunrise.

Through this process the etheric body is "siphoned" out of the physical body, and the thread of consciousness that binds one's awareness to the physical body is severed. In this way the etheric double is separated from the material body. This thread of consciousness, also called the silver thread (Ecclesiastes: 12,6), is a thread of ether that during life is bound to the physical body. When the etheric body withdraws from the physical body in the dying process, a highly sensitive person might be aware of a bluish-white-violet vapor which thickens to a form that is the exact double of the dying person.

At the moment of death the silver thread is severed, so that the spiritual life form separates from the material body. The earthly form is laid aside. At first the consciousness of the dead person is in the etheric body as the physical body begins to disintegrate. Everyone has an etheric double. The main function of this etheric body is to protect the physical body. It permeates and surrounds the physical body, even extending beyond it by some one to two inches. Our planet also has a comparable protective shield, which we call the ozone layer. It protects every living thing on the earth from the life-threatening rays of the sun.

Ether

In physics the term "ether" (Greek *aitaer*, blue heaven) refers to a substance that has been determined to be 1.5×10^{11} times lighter than air. In physics one differentiates by grades of density: subatomic, ethereal, gaseous, fluid, solid.

Particles of all densities contribute to forming our bodies and are divided into two parts:

1) the physical body, consisting of dense, liquid, and gaseous substances (known as atomic); and

2) the etheric body or etheric double, consisting of etheric and subatomic material.

Albert Einstein gave a lecture about ether and the theory of relativity. One of his closing remarks was that tiny "bits" of ether are constantly appearing and disappearing, and that these "bits" cannot be traced through time as we know it. (Albert Einstein, "Ether and Relativity Theory," speech given on May 5, 1920 at the Reichs University in Leiden, Springer Publishing House, Berlin.)

The etheric cover itself is not the bearer of independent consciousness, though it is absolutely essential for a living physical body.

The etheric cover absorbs streaming particles from the sun and conducts them on to the physical body. This cover is an exact duplicate of the physical form, but extends beyond the skin. Sensitive people perceive it as a light, misty bluish-white aura.

The normal eye cannot detect this etheric cover, but it is of a purely physical nature and can be badly impaired by cold, heat, or acidity, by fear, anger, or accident. People who have had an amputation often complain about pain in the amputated limb. That is explainable because the etheric body remains intact until death.

The etheric cover protects us from cosmic rays, which, unfiltered, could penetrate the physical body and cause harm.

The etheric cover has two main functions:

1) It absorbs subatomic particles, which give us energy. In the Indian spiritual tradition this vital energy is called *prana* or life-energy. It flows into the body through our energy centers.

2) It builds a bridge between the physical and the astral body, between the third and fourth dimensions.

Once the etheric body withdraws from the physical body, one's whole life passes in review like a fast-forwarded film. One sees everything that happened through or with oneself in a very short time, like a panorama, event for event; the successes as well as the failures, one's loving and gentleness, one's hatred, desires, abilities and inabilities. One recognizes the determining thoughts that accompanied one through life, and experiences for oneself the pain one caused, as well as the joy and love one gave to others. It is written in the Upanishads, the holy scriptures of the Hindus, that the etheric body carries all the information acquired during life on earth and gives it over to the divine.

As soon as the etheric body has withdrawn from the physical body, and life energy can no longer flow, the body begins to disintegrate.

At first the etheric body doesn't go very far from the physical body, but hovers over it. For a short while, the dead person rests in peaceful quiet, but then, within a few minutes, the etheric body shakes itself free. There are, however, cases where the etheric body remains stuck in the physical body for hours, days, weeks, or even months. The reason for this will be dealt with in the chapter entitled "The Stray Soul." Within a short period after physical death, it is normal and natural for the etheric body to be discarded and the spiritual being becomes aware of being in his astral body. You could say that he awakens in the astral dimension of the spiritual world. Thus one might say, "death is a process of divesting."

In Summary

- » A person goes through the process of dying and dies. Life energy, also called prana, no longer flows through his physical body.

- » One's consciousness leaves the physical body and is in the etheric double for several minutes or hours and sometimes for weeks or months.

- » Normally, the spiritual being divests his etheric body within two hours to two days.

- » One's consciousness now awakens in the astral body. A change in consciousness has taken place.

Depending on one's spiritual evolution, sooner or later the astral body will also be divested (see the chapter "The Transition Zone").

Four

Prolonged or Sudden Death Due to Severe Illness

A person who knows he is going to die from a severe illness such as cancer normally passes through five stages. Elizabeth Kübler-Ross has conducted remarkable research, studying and analyzing the dying process of many ill persons. In her book *Interviews with the Dying*[8] she describes the succession of phases that terminally ill people pass through.

1. Denial — The fact that death is near is rejected. Adverse information is negated or disputed.
2. Anger and revolt — The ill person finds his destiny unfair, and is often hostile toward the healthy.
3. Bargaining — For example, he offers God a deal: "If I get well, I will do such and such."
4. Deep depression — He realizes that death is inevitable.
5. Acceptance — He acknowledges the fact that death

is surrender and hope. He longs for a broader, new existence.

The greater the inner willingness to "give up" one's physical body, the easier it will be to open one's eyes to a new dimension in life!

Five

Caring for the Dying

It is extremely important that a sick person on his deathbed receive a particular kind of care. The spiritual attitude of the caregiver, relatives, and hospital staff are a part of this care. Caregivers are, so to speak, the midwives, helping a birth into a different dimension. Knowing this, it is appalling for a dying person to be treated indifferently. A loving, caring attitude means a great deal for the dying, because it makes passing over so much easier.

 At the moment of death, it is a great gift to be surrounded by love and acceptance, by flowers, light, and a comforting atmosphere. It is the task of the living and healthy to help the dying person to accept his approaching death, to soothe his fears, pain, and disorientation, and to treat him with dignity, since he will take this final impression of earthly life into the next dimension. This is exactly what the work of the Hospice Organization makes possible. Naturally, it is best when the old or ill person can remain in his own home, surrounded by the people he loves. If the dying person is religious, it is wonderful when visitors or relatives pray with him. Pictures might be hung on the wall that have a positive spiritual message, for example, a picture of Saint Francis of Assisi speaking to the animals, or a picture depicting the Mother of God and her loving helpfulness. Pictures of angels and saints that have a joyful mood should be chosen. Music that the dying person loves and inspiring books on tape are also supportive.

On the first visit to someone who is dying, it is advisable to build trust. One begins by talking about things in general and asking questions. The visitor mostly listens. Only after trust has been established can one let the dying person know that one is not afraid to speak about death. Death is a birth into a different life. The physical body is laid aside like a dress, and a new life begins on a different, finer vibrational level. Help that an attendant can give sometimes consists merely in listening, focusing one's full attention on the worries, fears, and wishes of the dying person, without reassuring her or thinking of changing anything. At this point words will hardly ease the situation. It is far more important that the dying person feel comforted, that her feelings are accepted, that she feels she can cry without being hushed, and is allowed to be afraid, because the path before her sometimes seems far too long and strenuous. "Through my attentive listening and my undivided attention and respect, through my being there and staying there, I am helpful — not through imparting some 'appropriate' words. At the hour of death, not much doing is needed."[9]

A mistake that relatives and children often make is to lie to the dying person. He knows in his soul that he will die. However, his ego-self might not yet be in agreement, and he asks, "Do you think I will recover?" Only too often the relatives, though they suspect or even know that it isn't going to happen, answer, "You'll soon be up and walking around again." These lies bear witness to one's own fear and inability to deal with "going home" in a natural way. Actually, the term "going home" is a wonderful description, signaling security and peace. We are going home to a place that we are actually already familiar with, that is waiting for us, where we feel good. Home is where we experience deep love and true peace. It is the place of eternal light where our real being can reveal itself. It is far from all the confusion of the material world, which only revolves around striving to increase wealth and recognition. It is the place of true beauty, which lies hidden in the human soul, which outlasts death, and where one discovers God's joy that one has come home. Homecoming means returning to the place where one loves and is loved. One has to have once gone away to appreciate the meaning of coming home.

Witness Report

Grisha's mother had business to attend to on the weekend, and asked her parents to take care of her eight-year-old son.

Grisha was happy to be with his grandparents, and asked his grandfather to help him learn how to ride a bicycle. Grisha's grandfather practiced with him the whole afternoon, helping his grandson climb back on the small bicycle again and again. Finally Grisha was able to balance and ride without help.

Happy and proud, he said, "Grandfather, I can ride a bicycle, and now I am going home." His grandfather answered, "Grisha, your mother is not coming until tomorrow morning, and then she will come and get you. Today you are still staying with us."

"No, Grandfather," answered the boy, "today I am going home." He went into the bedroom he shared with his grandfather, lay down on the bed, fell asleep, and died with a smile on his face.

—Martina from Hamlin

It is important to know that the time of death is never determined by chance but rather by the soul. It is the higher, spiritual, eternal part of man and is in close contact and communication with both the divine and the outwardly oriented, active, feeling and thinking part of the person. The soul sends the earthly personality impulses and inwardly prepares him. The trouble today is that few people are conscious of their souls and, as a result, they are unable to consciously recognize impulses from their own souls. Death occurs when the higher self of an older or severely ill person acknowledges that it makes no sense to remain in a physical body on this earth. This point in time can be sooner or later than the person's outer consciousness might wish.

The Most Important Considerations In Accompanying the Process of Dying

- » Strive to be quiet and understanding.
- » Acknowledge the dignity of every person.
- » Once a basis of trust is established, speak naturally about death and going home.
- » Orange-colored light in the room supports the process of letting go (candles, votive lights, or a small orange-colored light bulb).
- » Praying together; relatives and other visitors can pray silently or aloud.
- » Burning sandalwood has a positive influence on the departing soul. However, not everyone likes this scent.
- » If you are staying in a room with a dying person, have peaceful, blessing thoughts.

- Play soft music that the dying person likes.
- Hang pictures in the room that are uplifting and encouraging.
- A dying person's room is his birthplace into a new dimension.
- Divine grace always places an angel at the side of the dying one to assure that the passing over is as easy as possible.
- Relatives are important through their presence, not through their words.

Prayers for the dying can be found at the end of this book.

A Candlelight Ritual at the Bedside

If the dying person is religious

Light three candles one after the other and say:

"I light this candle so that God's light will shine within you. God is the beginning and the end.

I light this candle so that the God's love may be complete in you. God's love is everywhere: in you, around you, over you, under you, next to you.

I light this candle so that joy may spread throughout you, that you may be comforted and granted peace. May the peace of God be with you."

If the dying person is not religious

"I light this candle for you, may it give you strength and light, strength and light for you.

I light this candle for you, may it give you love, love for you.

I light this candle for you, may it give you patience, patience for you.

These three candles are burning that you may have peace."

When many relatives and friends are present

On a table at the foot of the bed, light as many candles as there are people present, and give one to each of them. Facing the dying person and looking into his eyes, each one says:

"May the peace of God fill you. May the love of God surround you," and then places the candle on the table. There can be soft music in the background. At the end all sing a song together that the dying person wishes to hear. They can also pray together with the rosary.

If the Dying Person Is in a Coma

In our society it is little known that a person in coma up to his death can hear well with both his physical as well as with his etheric ears, for hearing is the last sense that a dying person loses.

So it is still possible to say goodbye and to impart words of love. It is also an opportunity to give thanks for the times shared in life. "I thank you, my beloved partner (my mother, my father, my child, my friend) that I had the good fortune to share my life with you." Perhaps in the quiet of the room, it is also the appropriate moment to ask and to give forgiveness. "Please forgive me for any conscious or unconscious pain and suffering I caused you. And I forgive you for any pain and suffering that you consciously or unconsciously caused me."

Now accompany the one lying in coma by breathing together with him at his rhythmic pace. This establishes a deep bond and tender exchange. Stroke his hands or his cheeks. Allow yourself time to stroke him or her with all the love in your heart.

Forgiveness

Look at the dying person and try to change your perception of her. You now have the choice to forgive and to decide to love. Your lower self might perhaps want to say, "You bad person. You have hurt me, I cannot forgive you." Don't we all know the mood of condemning? But quietly in your heart, there is also a voice that is saying, "Yes, I have been hurt, but I was not so nice to you either. Neither of us feels good." Simply be aware of what happened. It is not necessary to judge it. Just think about it.

Mistakes are as much a part of life as is forgiving. Wanting to destroy the other person or nurturing feelings of revenge are the wrong way. Whenever we feel angry or afraid, whenever we feel mistreated, there is also something that we can be grateful for. When Jesus was asked how often we should forgive, he answered, "…seventy times seven" (Matthew 18:21-22), which means again and again. Even when there is no more time for reconciliation or for the dying person to be reconciled with his perceived enemy, the belated act of forgiveness has great significance nonetheless. In the Catholic tradition there is the Last Anointment and the sacrament of confession, which give immense relief to many on their deathbeds.

By not forgiving, the etheric body becomes darker and denser. This density hinders higher, finer vibrations from permeating the physical body. Unwillingness to forgive, as in revenge or jealousy, makes the etheric body denser and it becomes much harder to shake off after death. Those who are generous of spirit and readily forgive can quickly release the etheric body after death.

Six

Death from the Perspective Of Those Left Behind

Having to accept the death of a loved one is an experience of deep suffering. For those left behind there is always a period of mourning, and its intensity depends on their spiritual attitude. The first phase is one of great pain, especially when those left behind were not prepared for it, as for example, with an accident or other kind of sudden death. The shock is not as great when it follows a long, drawn-out illness, but the loss is still painful. The second phase is one of denial. One doesn't accept it, can't believe that it is true. Then comes anger or depression, until the fact is finally accepted. Each phase lasts an undetermined length of time. Some people suffer deep depression for a year or two. The loss of a loved one can throw those left behind into feelings of helplessness and great despair, because in Western society the belief in the finality of death is so widely accepted. During our lifetimes we "exile" death, and therefore, when it does knock at the door, the shock is that much greater. To grieve well is of unimaginable value. We must know that mourning is more than sorrow. Mourning needs space, rituals, forms, and cultural as well as social parameters.[10]

~ Witness Report ~

Jutta: The funeral is over. The people who helped us through this difficult time have gone back to their daily lives. We experience an infinite emptiness in ourselves, in our house: the finality of it all — no more hugs, no more "hellos." What to do with the feeling of helplessness, the homesickness? "My God, show us a way to bear this loss!"

A nun directed me to a group that sang praises. Singing songs of praise and psalms over and over with the group (strange for me in the beginning), I threw all my pain, anger, and sorrow at God. Then I felt so free. The stillness afterward filled me with quietude and deep peace. Joining them for an hour each week became the saving grace for me. Gradually I built up the energy to live my daily life again, learning not to repress my pain and sorrow, but to accept them, as held by God. Stillness and singing praises had a great healing effect on me. This path renewed my deep joy for life and protected me from feeling that everything was senseless."

Sigi: "Some months after the death of Jens, we heard about a group in our neighborhood that regularly met to practice meditative dance. Jutta and I went there together. From the very first I experienced a sense of being included in the group, of being held by them. Music had always been meaningful to me, but here the combination of movement and gestures became a healing whole. In the ensuing period, the circle dance conducted around a center point became very important for me. I began to take an advanced course in meditative/sacramental dance, and after some time — and it wasn't just happenstance — the leader of the group asked me to take over. More than ten years of this way of dancing, with its different forms of expression and moods, helped me resolve my sorrow. But I wasn't the only one who found support there. Other dancers who were also facing the same or similar circumstances were given a foothold and comfort through my continued leadership of the circle dance."

—Jutta and Sigi from Uhldingen

In the village where I was born, it was the custom to bid farewell to the deceased. One went to where the body lay, stood before it, and said something friendly. In Baden-Wuerttemberg (Germany) the body may be kept at home for thirty-six hours or kept for viewing in a funeral home. In other countries the laws may, of course, be different.

After the physical death of a loved one, many relatives are in a state of overwhelming shock, are benumbed, or emotionally churned up. Their balance between body and soul is disturbed, and they often weep uncontrollably.

Because he cannot comfort them, this deeply saddens the dead person, who can see and is experiencing the whole scene from a different perspective.

Until the burial, the soul of the dead person stays in the immediate proximity of his relatives and beloved friends. He wants to comfort them and communicate through fine vibrations and gestures, "I am not dead, I am alive; I have only laid aside my physical body." However, often these souls are unable to make themselves felt, because those left behind are wrapped in a dark cloud of pain.

Seven

Death from the Perspective Of the Deceased

Here are some examples of near-death experiences and witness reports.

Witness Report

Frank, in Berlin, reports about his near-death experience. He had been declared dead, but suddenly awoke and remembered this experience in great detail. It changed his life dramatically.

"My God, I am floating above my body, am I possibly dead? Oh, my God, I see my body stretched out under a white cloth.

Everyone around me thinks that I am dead, but I am not dead. I am not. People are crying. Please listen to me. Please stop. I am not dead, I'm here, I'm alive. Why can't you see me?

The doctor is comforting my wife and my mother. I'm trying to tell my wife that I'm okay, that my suffering is over, that I can move my body freely. I want her to hear me, but no one is listening."

Diary Entry

Heinz: "My wife doesn't feel my presence. I have no way of getting her attention. What is going on?"

Guide: "Can't you see that she is consumed with grief? She is suffering from a shock, because for her, you are dead. See the dark energy around her? She is numbed, a prisoner of her pain."

Heinz: "She should stop crying and look at me, then maybe I can connect with her. It saddens me that I am right next to her, touching her, and she doesn't notice. I love her so much. Karin, look at me."

Guide: "Come with me, let's go into another zone. Later you can see your wife again. Let us go away for a while, as it will make things easier for you."

Heinz: "No, no. I want to stay here. I won't go until she at least feels that I am here. I want so much to comfort her. How can I do that? Isn't there anything I can do that will help her?"

Guide: "At the moment there is no way for you to reach her. Let your love energy flow to her, and then, hopefully, she will calm down."

Heinz: "That is not easy for me, because I am so upset."

Guide: "Send her loving thoughts and then come with me. In a while we will return here. She will have calmed down, and *your loving thoughts will be able to reach her. Now it is time to go, we will come back later."*

Witness Report

"All my life I felt that I had been wearing a costume without knowing it. Then one day the costume dropped from me, and I recognized what I had been the whole time. I wasn't what I had thought I was. My whole life I had thought that I was a person, a body. I thought, *I am so and so, a woman, a mother, a secretary, and so on.* As I entered the other world, I discovered that I had always been something entirely different. I was a soul and not a body. I could neither die nor be born. I was eternal. I was neither a woman nor a man. It was like waking up after a spell of amnesia. I was happy to be "me" again. It had always been me, but I had lost sight of that and had thought I was a physical body. My body was only the outer clothing that I needed for my life here on the earth. When I was finished with it, then I would be free of it."[11]

Witness Report

"I felt as if I were floating, and I heard wonderful sounds. Additionally, I was aware of parallel harmonious movements and colors. Somehow I had the feeling that I was not alone. Yet I saw no one. A divine peace and an inner harmony I had never felt before filled my consciousness. I was totally happy and not burdened by any problems. I was alone. No earthly being, neither parents, wife, children, friends, nor enemies disturbed my divine rest. All I had was a clear sensation: "Nearer my God to Thee..." I floated up, closer and closer to the light."[12]

Everyone who dies experiences this transition somewhat differently; however, the many accounts of near-death experiences have remarkable similarities.

» Many remember moving through a tunnel at the end of which was a radiant light. Nearly all of them went toward the light. For a few, the light moved toward them.

» Some people don't see the tunnel, but immediately see the place where they left their physical bodies. This usually happens when there has been an accident. They look down on the scene, the doctors, the ambulance, and then on their relatives.

» Some describe floating up through a misty cloud. Then they see their relatives. Almost all these souls feel uplifted, happy, in harmony, floating, expansive, and free of problems.

» Often, spiritual guides, angels, or relatives who have already died come to accompany the soul being. At first, most of the dead feel the need to comfort and calm their loved ones who are still in shock and full of pain.

Eight

How Souls Make Contact With Those Still on Earth

It is very important for those who have died to help and console their beloved relatives. These souls are no longer tied down by the body's heaviness. They are free from attitudes and the controlling influence of one-sided intellectual thought. What they want to show and say is: "Look, I am alive." Some souls are so enthusiastic about being able to help their relatives that it is a real joy for them when their work shows effect. Unfortunately, we Western materialists have lost the capacity we once had for building bridges between the lower, denser vibrations of our three-dimensional world and the higher, finer vibrational dimensions. It seems almost impossible for most of us to even imagine that there can be something like healing contact.

Again and again the dead are most concerned with convincing those in grief that their loved one is, as always, alive and doing well. It would be much easier for those in sorrow to deal with their loss if they were to realize that the absence of their loved one is only due to a changed level of reality rather than a loss forever. The soul's influence should encourage those left behind to not despair, but rather to bring more spirituality into their own lives.

How do the souls of the dead seek to make contact with those left behind? This can happen in the following ways:

Physical contact;
An overflow of energy;
Wonderful scents;
Resonating tones;
Meeting through a dream;
Through children;
Through pets;
Messages from angels.

Physical Contact — A soul who wishes to contact a physically alive person looks at the energy pattern and energy field of the person she wants to comfort. She studies it very carefully to see where in the body the energy pattern is in harmony; for example, in the head or the arm, the heart or the stomach region, or in the individual chakras. It is important to bring the spirit of the sender into harmony with that of the receiver, so that a loving transfer can take place. The soul sends a gentle ray of thought energy to the most receptive zone. Generally there is an emotional and positive reaction. The mourner suddenly feels relieved. While he doesn't know what happened, a much lighter feeling often convinces him that his beloved one who died is alive.

An Overflow of Energy — While the soul is hovering over beloved relatives and directly confronted with their pain, he concentrates energy, focuses it, and sends it to the beloved.

Diary Entry

Guide: "Why are you here in your relatives' house?"

Lisa: "I want to contact my mother. She is so alone now."

Guide: "How are you going to contact her?"

Lisa: "I am directing a stream of energy directly to her back. I have already had success doing that."

Guide: "And what success was that?"

Lisa: "My mother is so desperate that I want to send her a sign that I am still with her. I put all my love into a concentrated beam of energy. She reacts to it."

Guide: "How do you do it?"

Lisa: "I concentrate the energy through my thoughts and my love. Then I concentrate on her back or her head and flood her with this focused energy."

Guide: "How do you know that she reacts to it? What does her reaction look like?"

Lisa: "My mother is so blocked by her pain and so withdrawn. After I sent the energy to her, she sits up straight. Often she looks in my direction and smiles. That's how I can see that it is good for her."

Wonderful Scents — Sometimes, during the period of mourning, those left behind become aware of a wonderful scent and think of the dead person at the very same time. There are some scents that partners shared together while both were alive, that they found particularly beneficial, for example, the inimitable smell of a fir forest in the early morning.

Perhaps the couple loved the sea with its typical ocean smell or the smell of an open fire spurs an unforgettable memory, a specific experience associated with it. Personally, I find the scent of some roses incredibly wonderful. I often say to my husband, "Smell this, isn't it overwhelming?" He bends over the rose and both of us sniff the priceless flower again and feel the gift of the rose's perfume.

Diary Entry

"I was unable to reach my wife Sybille. Her deep sadness made it very difficult, and the openness she had had earlier wasn't there anymore. From another spirit in my present level, I learned how to concentrate energy, so that it became noticeable as a scent in the physical ether. When I tried this

technique, my wife reacted immediately. Whenever I created this scent, she thought of me immediately and knew that I was there. That made me very happy!"

— Account from a deceased husband

Resonating Tones — In all the years during which I shared my thoughts about life and death with others, I frequently heard gripping stories from survivors about sudden tones and singing that moved them to tears and convinced them that their lost loved one was still there. Also, sometimes at the exact moment of death or passing into a new realm both the dying and their relatives hear beautiful singing or harmonious tones.

Witness Report

Jutta's mother had lain dying for some time. The elderly woman was bedridden, and one evening she felt as if her last hour had come. She called her daughter, but Jutta was so absorbed in a TV program that she didn't hear her.

The mother increasingly sensed that it was almost time for her to cross the threshold, and her deepest wish was to say goodbye to Jutta, to embrace her. She prayed to God from the depths of her heart, "Oh my God, grant me my wish, and send an angel to Jutta to bring her to my bedside."

Just at that moment, as the dying woman prayed, Jutta heard

beautiful singing at her front door. She jumped up and went immediately to the entrance, but found nothing. Because she was so certain that she had heard singing, she went to the patio door, but again she neither heard nor saw anything. Then she ran upstairs to her mother who told her then how intensely she had prayed and how much she had wished that her daughter would come to her. Then Jutta's mother fell asleep forever in her daughter's arms.

—Jutta from Hamlin told me this story with tears in her eyes.

Meeting through a Dream — Some time ago I spoke about death with a woman from Bulgaria. She told me that it is the custom in her country, some days after the death of a loved one, to ask the relatives, "Have you dreamed about him yet?" When the answer is yes, it means the soul of the dead one has arrived home in the sphere of light. Once there, these souls often are glad to use dreams to communicate with their loved ones. We who are physically alive are much more receptive while asleep than we are when awake. Sometimes, when we awake we know that we have experienced something beautiful, though we can't remember it exactly. At other times, we have a fleeting impression of something that quickly fades, leaving us with vague fragments that soon vanish and cannot be recalled. There are, however, times when we remember extremely vivid impressions from dreams for quite a while.

In general, dreams can be sorted into the following categories:

1. Dreams that bring relief — The many unordered thoughts and feelings of the day surface from the subconscious and are worked through in dreams, relieving deep-seated stress.

2. Dreams that solve problems — Certain dream sequences appear that can be understood symbolically when one awakens. Often, paths that aid in spiritual growth are indicated.

3. Spiritual dreams — Helpers, soul teachers, masters, angels, and soul companions appear as messengers carrying new impulses that encourage the dreamer in his spiritual development.

A soul spirit on a higher astral plane is also capable of imparting knowledge and information by impressing it upon the physical brain. An ethereal bridge is built between the astral sphere and the physical world, so that pictures can be received in the physical brain. The more receptive the brain is to the vibrations of finer bodies, the easier the transfer will be.

Through Children — Some souls choose children as messengers for communication. Children are not so conceptually warped in how they think. Until they are seven or eight, their bridges to the spiritual world function much better than we adults suspect. Particularly within their own families, small children can be excellent messengers, and in the future we will learn from them more and more frequently. In the book *I Come from the Sun*,[13] two Argentinean children, Flavio and his brother, Marcos, remember what it was like before they had physical bodies. They talk repeatedly about things that shake their parents' view of the world:

"I had a wonderful and special dream, which didn't seem like a dream at all. I found myself in front of a house with a garden full of unusual flowers that don't exist here. I rang and a large door opened. As I went in I lost consciousness. A girlfriend, who was very beautiful and had violet light flowing around her, lifted me up. She gave me some of her energy. The energy was light. She brought me to another place. Our grandparents were there with all of us. We filled ourselves with light and light was all around us. I didn't want to leave, and I still long to go back to that special place. I believe that is where we dwell before our births and return after our deaths. We can also go there in our dreams. On awakening, we always have to come back to this life, but I believe that that special place is actually reality."

Diary Entry

Guide: "How do you contact your wife?"

Rene: "I direct my energy directly to her heart. She is very depressed by my death and cries a lot."

Guide: "Are you successful with your method?"

Rene: "Unfortunately not. I can't reach her. It is a dilemma. I so want to comfort her. But now I will turn my attention to my daughter Lilly. Perhaps she will notice me."

Guide: "Why do you believe that Lilly will be able to better sense your presence?"

Rene: "I love my daughter so much and believe that we have a deep relationship with each another."

Guide: "What do you want to communicate to Lilly?"

Rene: "I want her to know only that I am not dead, and I want to tell her farewell."

Guide: "Do you also want to reach your daughter with a ray of thought energy?"

Rene: "Yes, I want to send the energy to her feet and to kiss her feet. That's what I always did when I put her to bed."

Guide (after a pause): "Were you successful?"

Rene: "Yes, Lilly giggled and smiled. She looked in my direction. I wished her farewell. I am certain she will not forget the experience."

Guide: "Will Lilly tell her mother about it?"

Rene: "I hope so. That would be wonderful."

Through Pets — Animals communicate on a different level than we human beings. They send pictures, gestures, and display various demeanors. If one is willing to try, they can be transformed into words. Cats and dogs, in particular, have the ability to see the dead. They frequently announce them by barking, meowing, or acting in an atypical way.

I remember often walking with my dog, Canda, along the edge of a forest. Whenever we reached a specific spot, the hair on the back of her neck stood up and she refused to go any farther along the small footpath. Every time, she ran off in panic, made a huge curve around the spot, and then waited for me many yards ahead on the same path. I was quite amazed by this behavior. Some time later a farmer told me that he never took his horse there, on principle, because it always shied and refused to stay on the path. So then I began to ask the villagers whether something special had happened there in the past. No one knew the answer. Some years later I was given an old, out-of-print book about the village and its history. In it was written that that precise spot was where court cases were heard, and those found guilty were hanged right there.

Witness Report

An older woman told this story about her beautiful Siamese cat.

"My husband of forty-two years died two weeks ago. I'm sure it is hard for you to imagine what it is like to be old and alone, left without your partner of so many years. I feel so awfully lonely. Then, two days ago, something very strange happened. It was 3:50 a.m. Normally, my cat, Tina, sleeps beside me in bed and stays there until morning. But on that night, she meowed very loudly on the staircase and kept looking at the wall and then at me. A wonderful, happy feeling flowed through me, and suddenly I knew that my husband was standing there. I said, "Johannes, is that you?" My heart was pounding, and it seemed to me that I could actually feel Johannes's presence. This experience transformed my life and my pain into the certainty that Johannes can sometimes be here with me. Tina helped me realize this."

Messages from Angels — Angels are God's messengers. Every religion mentions them, though the names might be different. The Greek word *angelos* means "he who is sent." In Hebrew there is a word *malach* that also means messenger. In Buddhism and Hinduism angels are called devas or dralas. The Bible speaks of angels and archangels, the mighty and the powerful. In the Christian tradition, knowledge of guardian angels and archangels is also widespread.

The names of the four most important archangels are familiar to us:

Michael — He is as God;
Gabriel — The ruler over the earth;
Raphael — The shining one who heals;
Uriel — The fire of God.

At the end of each archangel's name we hear the last syllable "el" which tells us the angel's origin. "El" is from the Hebrew and means "out of God." When we ask angels to help us, they give us vibrations of pure light. They wrap those calling for help in the pure light of their unconditional love. If one's physical or etheric body is too dense or too dark, then it is hard to feel this healing vibration.

Angels can have enormous influence on our spiritual, mental, emotional, and physical states. They can take on any shape or form in order to help humans and animals in a most wonderful and comforting way. They are pure, unconditional love, and they bring this love to us as often as we call upon them.

These angelic beings have the purest thoughts and feelings. They are unfamiliar with negative traits as we know them. They feel no anger, impatience, or ill-tempered moods, and they are neither resentful nor condescending. For angels it is difficult to work together with us human beings. For one thing, it is not always easy for humans to recognize them, so they are often not understood. Also, they are constantly ironing out the many mistakes humans make. If a person is open to the angels' finer vibrations, he will notice that angels are always nearby — in prayer — when a child is born, when someone is dying, whenever a person exudes goodwill and harmony to his surroundings.

Witness Report

"One morning, as I lay still but awake in bed, I suddenly saw a large, bright being of light standing before me. I knew immediately that it was an angel of God. It stood, radiant, and said, "Your friend Hilde is well; she has just this moment come home." Actually, the angel didn't speak with audible words, but even so I heard them very clearly in my mind. Hilde had cancer, and the angel gave me the message at the exact moment she died. Later that afternoon I heard from her relatives that she had died in Cairo in the early morning hours.

—Hanna from Dortmund

Nine

Help Through Soul Guides And Relatives Who Have Already Crossed the Threshold

We've all experienced enchanting sunsets — hues of gold and orange, shades of blue and white, blending and merging into one another. Many of us are fascinated by these beautiful sunsets, gazing at them with complete devotion over and over again. We also know that there are sunsets that are dominated by dark clouds, so that the fabulous display of color remains invisible. Just like one of nature's sunsets, we can look upon death as a sunset, one that can be experienced as beautiful, peaceful, and harmonious, or alternatively, as clouded by dark thoughts.

Of course no one can say exactly how another person experiences this "sunset," whether they see darkness and gray or recognize the brilliant display of colors. It depends on which thoughts and feelings they have as they change planes, which love frequency vibrates in their cells. A person with a high love frequency is, in the realm of his etheric heart, so advanced that he is able to experience what happens in other dimensions. While still living here, he already deeply knows, "I am held and embraced by the love of God." In complete trust the soul knows, "In my Father's house are many dwellings."

As long as thinking about death causes only anxiety and fear, it is quite understandable that thoughts of dying and death are suppressed. Under such circumstances it is impossible to be prepared for the event. It may happen that such a person, by virtue of his dark consciousness created through fear, depression, panic, attachment to the earthly, or an unforgiving attitude, misses one of the most beautiful experiences ever — a sunset of endless blazing color!

During the dying process, close relatives who have passed on, or soul guides, among them the angels, are waiting on the other side. While they were alive, soul guides were highly developed teachers, ready to support a soul on the verge of passing to make a healthy adjustment to the new dimension. With their help, the new orientation is made easier and a harmonious balance can be found. Although sometimes immediately after death it may seem that no one is present, we are nonetheless not left to our own resources. At the moment of crossing over we are awaited and welcomed. People who were important to us during our life on earth are always ready to receive us "at the gate."

Diary Entry

Guide: "You have arrived and have already acclimatized yourself a bit. How are you?"

Frank: "It is so easy here, so spacious, so consoling. I feel warm and protected. I'm not thinking of those I left behind anymore. It is wonderful how light I feel. Everything seems so familiar."

Guide: "Look around, do you see anyone?"

Frank: "You are the only one I can see, but I have the feeling that there is someone else here." Frank looks around and then shortly afterward says, "I see energy fields that are moving."

Guide: "How are the energy fields moving?"

Frank: "They come toward me and then they seem to dissolve. They're floating, I think. I can't tell exactly, but in my mind I feel that something familiar is there."

Guide: "While you are looking at the energy fields, try to feel what you can perceive of them."

Frank: "Oh, it's... it's... yes, it's my grandfather, it really is him!" Frank begins to laugh and cry. He and his grandfather greet each other heartily. Some time later, "Now I see other people. They are standing in the background. They are a little blurry, farther away, but I feel that I know them all."

Guide: "If you want to, you can go to them. It would be nice for you to recognize them."

Frank: "Oh, my God, it's you, Rose. I can hardly believe that I am seeing you again. What a joy!" Frank immerses himself completely in this moment of recognition. He is reunited with his wife, who had predeceased him. The guide sees two compact energy fields of brilliant light spiraling round each other. One can tell how they are expressing their joy. Then the two share a quiet, intimate conversation.

Guide: "How lovely that you are all together again. Was your grandfather an important figure for you?"

Frank: "Yes, it is so good to be together again. My grandfather was and is my soul guide. He helped me while alive to follow the spiritual path. I love him very, very deeply, as I do my wife Rose."

Within the framework of a study, British scientists examined heart attack patients who had been declared clinically dead but were revived.

88% experienced an overwhelming feeling of happiness.

72% saw or thought they saw Christ or an angel.

69% saw their lives run by as if on film.

44% experienced a tunnel.

44% were told that it was not yet the right time for them to die.

33% described the experience as if "they had come home."

22% saw a beam of light.

12% experienced darkness.

Source: www.expeditionzone.com

There is something great within you.
Is it your talent?
Is it your feelings?
Is it your immeasurable reserve of power and energy?
Is it your memories?
Is it your heart?
Is it your intellect?
Is it your awareness?
Is it your subconscious?
Is it your intelligence?
Yes, what is it that is great about you?

The greatness in you is so strong
That nothing can be compared to it.
You, the soul, are the greatness in you.
This greatness is not an object, nor a person.
It is beyond your imagination,
Beyond your thinking and emotions.
The greatness in you is your everlasting existence.
The awareness of your eternal godliness,
That is at the same time unconditional love.
It never dies.
It is — you are — pure being.
You are eternal existence, eternal consciousness, eternal love,
Eternal mercy, joy,
Unutterable holiness in your innermost being.
The soul is the innermost essence of love.

Ten

The Transition Zone

Everyone who has died and arrives at the gate to the spiritual world has laid aside the thick veil, the physical body, and now lives as a soul in a finer, more sensitive, lighter robe. Now he or she can see and enter into the next higher sphere and dimension.

I would like to use an example to illustrate this. Water can have differing degrees of density, such as ice, liquid, or steam. Still, the substance consists only of water molecules. That is what it is like with the soul's "robes." Sometimes it dresses itself with "ice," "water," or "steam" — that is, in different forms.

Like a fingerprint, each soul has its own unique composition, its own particular vibrational radiance. Nonetheless, it cannot be defined as a body, for then the soul would be a form limited by boundaries. The enveloping veils are merely energy fields, limited and changeable. For me, the soul is essential nature from the Source, from God's heart.

When the physical body dies, the soul lives on in a more refined robe. This is more permeable, more transparent, more adaptable, and much more mobile than our human bodies. The soul reveals itself now — symbolically speaking — in its water robe. This robe, too, dissolves within a few days. Then the soul lives in a yet finer robe, the consistency of mist. The soul always remains the soul just as water molecules remain water molecules regardless of their state. So the soul can wear many robes, until in the end it has laid them all aside and recognizes itself for what it really is: the pure essence of unconditional Love.

At the physical level the soul can only manifest itself in a limited way. The closer the soul comes to its source, the more intensively it can realize the dimensions of its being. We, as souls aware of our selves, can experience many dimensions, and every dimension is a different aspect of our selves. The fourth dimension, the astral world described in this book, is different from the fifth or sixth, and different again from the seventh, eighth, or ninth dimensions. We humans are nine-dimensional beings and can, depending on our consciousness or higher consciousness, experience these levels either simultaneously or successively. However, all dimensions — there are more than nine — exist within the pure potential, the source essence, the eternal unity with the Father.

After the soul has laid aside the physical body, it first arrives in the transition zone (see diagram 2).

The soul is expected here, and experiences its new environment as warm and comforting. Everything appears to be light and much brighter. The tensions and worries that troubled it on earth have fallen away and a wonderful feeling of well-being surrounds the newborn soul. Here it floats or walks, stands or swirls around in a cloudlike bundle of finely vibrating energy. Depending on individual character and degree of consciousness, the soul will need more or less time to become accustomed to this new environment.

The first thing that the soul experiences after dying is layers of light of differing shades of white, waves of color and tones, fine and quiet bells, soft music, and a feeling of deep and comforting peace. Then the soul usually sees its soul guide or people it is close to, such as its spouse, parents, grandparents, siblings, uncles and aunts, dear friends, and sometimes — depending on maturity and consciousness — its guardian angel, angels, and saints. Besides this, the soul notices a wider panorama of differing layers of light, lines of light that bend and move in waving harmony, as if the light were living intelligence expressing itself through a wonderful display of color, in geometrical forms, and constantly changing hues, creating a landscape of lights of sublime beauty. All is in constant harmonious motion, directed by a light-filled spiritual power.

The Astral World or the 4th Dimension

1	*Learning Zone*	sphere of songs and prayers	Transparent white-gold
2	*Learning Zone*	contentment, openness, healing	Transparent violet
3	*Learning Zone*	forbearance, patience, harmonious beauty, creative power	Transparent blue
4	*Learning Zone*	harmonizes mankind, animals and plants	Transparent light green
5	*Learning Zone*	reflecting on and evaluating one's past life	Transparent light gray
	Transition Zone	entrance gate for every newborn at this level	
6	*Souls still bound to the Earth*	self-recognition and remorse	Gray
7	*Souls still bound to the Earth*	unconsciousness and confused souls	Black

7th astral level: Most dense level

Diagram 2

What takes place in the transition zone?

» In the loving presence of its soul guide, the soul will be surrounded by a bubble of light so that an uplifting feeling of closeness arises.

» The first transitional contact may be that either a soul guide or close friend directs a bright ray of light onto the newly arrived soul. Then the soul will be lovingly led home.

» Due to its own heaviness, the human soul initially does not accept these helping impulses and sinks into heavy, dense zones. In such cases, the soul guides work tirelessly to reach the confused soul.

» If a soul has died through a natural disaster, accident, war, or suicide, and is therefore at the door to the spiritual world in an unharmonious, contorted state, soul helpers perform emergency measures in the transition zone.

Diary Entry

Guide: "Can you describe exactly what you see and feel now that you have left the tunnel?"

Rose: "It is as if I'm floating or swimming in light, and I feel that I am being directed and carried by an invisible power. You are the first one that I see."

Guide: "Can you say where the invisible power is taking you?"

Rose: "I have the feeling that I am swimming homeward. Yes, it is as if I am swimming in a stream of energy."

Guide: "What does the stream of energy feel like?"

Rose: "Porous, warm.... It feels like I am in a harmony of thoughts consisting of a cloudlike substance. It is hard to describe it. I feel thoughts of love — as if others are waiting for me. But I don't see anything clearly."

Guide: "What else do you see? Look around. Perhaps you will see more clearly if you look more closely."

Rose: "I see spots of light. They are moving and spiraling around, but nothing with concrete forms. I see groups of fields of light. Oh, now I can see better... I thought I was alone with you.... Oh, my God... there's my mother. Oh, mother, I have missed you so!"

After they both have whirled around and tenderly greeted each other, Rose sees her mother and two dear friends standing close to her more clearly. The people most important to her in life are recognized first, while some other friends and relatives remain in the background. Those standing farther away are recognized after a period of becoming acclimated. That is because when one enters the fourth dimension, feelings and hearing are stronger senses than sight.

Diary Entry

Guide: "What do you feel and see now that you have passed through the tunnel into the light?"

Holger: "I am moving in a stream of light. I feel that the light is intelligent. I experience the light embracing me. It is so velvety and relaxed, full of trust. There is an understanding around me. Everything is simple, I know where I am and why I am here."

Guide: "Can you see what is around you? Do you see the other souls?"

Holger: "I am in a light stream of love. The light is like parents caressing me with their arms. Nothing has a concrete structure. Somehow I know that there are other souls here, too, but I don't see them. I sense that other beings are passing by me and are here, for no one is really isolated."

Guide: "What does the loving light sound like?"

Holger: "Everything is alive, the sounds are alive. Nothing is static, although you might think so at first. I hear light, soft and harmonious tones one after another, but I can also feel them, like a gentle touch. It is unbelievably wonderful. I feel and hear notes that I have never heard on earth. My whole being is expanding. The light is coming from every side. It carries all the sounds and frequencies of the universe and nonetheless I feel a deep stillness far beyond all silence. What a wonder, what peace, what love."

The wonder of life, of dying and of being born, has very little to do with the intellect. It is a process of eternal divine being. The intellect is a fantastic, brilliant instrument, but it has great difficulty trying to grasp or explain the processes of Being that occur in the higher dimensions. The heart, though, can sense and experience it the more it opens itself to unconditional love. We humans are fantastic light beings, our bodies consisting of condensed light, condensed love. It is a universe of incredible being, and in this body lives the soul, which is eternal. In life and in dying we always have the chance to recognize and experience the great wisdom in the unending stream of love.

Diary Entry

Guide: "Now that you have passed through the tunnel into this dimension, tell me what you are aware of."

Thomas: "I see a light and am intensely aware that I am dead. But oddly, I am alive! How strange that I can see you. Wait just a moment. I want to talk to you. I am so surprised to be alive."

Guide: "Relax and continue speaking while we let the light guide us."

Thomas: "Everything is transparent, but I see some outlines. I have to get used to them. Yes, those are other people, souls like me, with eyes that are radiating light. Their facial features are becoming clearer, I am starting to recognize them.

They are sending pictures to my consciousness telepathically. I hear their thoughts... the forms are changing... they are becoming clearer.... What is this? Oh, this can't be."

Guide: "What do you see?"

Thomas: "My wife, Toni... Toni...."

Two light bodies of brilliant light whirl around each other. They unite, they hold each other close and hug.

Guide: "What are you doing?"

Thomas: "What a joy to see my beloved wife again! We are hugging; we are simply embracing. It is so good, we are so happy, so fulfilled."

After the tunnel experience the soul floats toward the light. Two different processes then take place:

Phase 1

The soul floats through a transitional zone. It experiences the light as living intelligence and is consoled, full of peace and harmony. It senses a higher order that directs and guides everything. If the soul's energy experienced great suffering on earth through an accident, war, violence, murder, or through an experience that shocked it, and is therefore out of balance, then it is brought to a healing center. All the rooms and spaces are not physical in nature, but are rather of finer vibrations. It is very comforting to have guides, protecting souls, or close relatives around one. Souls that are spiritually evolved do not need help in orienting themselves. They pass through the transitional zone very quickly on their own.

Phase 2

The most important characteristic of this phase is waking up, awakening in the divine. The soul moves closer and closer to the point of concentrated light. It knows that it is not alone and is astonished to experience moving through this transition field of strong, concentrated light. It experiences deep stillness, a stillness beyond silence. It experiences eternity beyond infinity, and deep peace while at the same time endless expansion. It is aware of being in the center of creation, aware of its oneness with the wellspring. It experiences itself as pure, unsullied consciousness. This moment is eternity, beyond space and time as we know them. In this state of eternity the soul recognizes that the divine is pure, absolute consciousness. It understands that God is unending love in the experience of all life, is one with all life. His Being shines through the different forms and veils. It is in every plant, every animal, every human being, every soul. The soul awakes and sees what it truly is: eternity — love — pure being in God.

After this moment of awakening (which can last differing lengths of time, according to our earthly feeling for time), the soul begins to create forms. It no longer sees itself as essential love, but rather begins to build a new "outward" form now in the fourth dimension, the astral world. The light veils that encompass it are of thin, lightly woven light of various colors.

Diary Entry

Guide: "How did you experience your arrival in this transitional zone after you died in a wartime bombing?"

Teben: "The first thing I saw was a white being. At first I thought it was an angel. Then I saw that it was my mom."

Guide: "How did your mother react when you arrived? What did she say?"

Teben: "At first I was a bit confused, because my mom looked so young and so radiant. In the beginning she stayed some distance from me."

Guide: "Why was that?"

Teben: "My energy was very disharmonious. I was chopped into pieces and torn apart. Fear and anger weighed me down. Mom called to me from a distance, 'Come with me, I will bring you to the healing center.' She beckoned to me in a friendly way."

Guide: "Did you know immediately that you were physically dead and on a completely different level from where you had been on earth?"

Teben: "It was some time later that I reflected on the wonder that life is the pure ability to feel, to move, and to have a different, pulsing body. In my old body everything essential was there and now is here."

Guide: "So eternal life is not a mysterious supernatural affair, but an everlasting aspect of the soul's essence?"

Teben: "It is possible to hurt or destroy the physical form, but not our invisible bodies. Life changes its form and defies earthly research. The most overwhelming thing is knowing that no force on earth can destroy life."

Guide: "May I come back to your transition? Why did your mother keep some distance from you?"

Teben: "She didn't want to endanger herself through my damaged energy. She hasn't had sufficient experience to know how to cope yet."

Guide: "In what way has your poor condition gotten better?"

Teben: "I was brought to a place that is called the healing center. It is especially for newcomers, just right for those who have similarly shattered bodies like mine."

Guide: "How did you experience the healing?"

Teben: "I felt like I was enveloped in a swirl. Different ringing tones flowed into me, and everything moved as in a centrifuge. I felt an invisible intelligence working on me. It was a thoroughly soothing feeling. Spiraling, green, healing light touched my body, as if it were massaging me. During this *process it changed its color to gold, then white, and at the end blue. Mom was standing there the whole time smiling. It was all so calming and loving."*

Guide: *"What happened after the healing?"*

Teben: *"I could sense things more clearly and precisely, so that beside my mom I saw friends and other relatives. Mom came and stroked my face. My deepest wish is to work at the healing center, too."*

Guide: *"Do you sometimes think about your life on earth and the war in which you lost your physical life?"*

Teben: *"What incomprehensible and unnecessary pain and nonsense. I will try to help my friends."*

Soul Group = Primary Group →

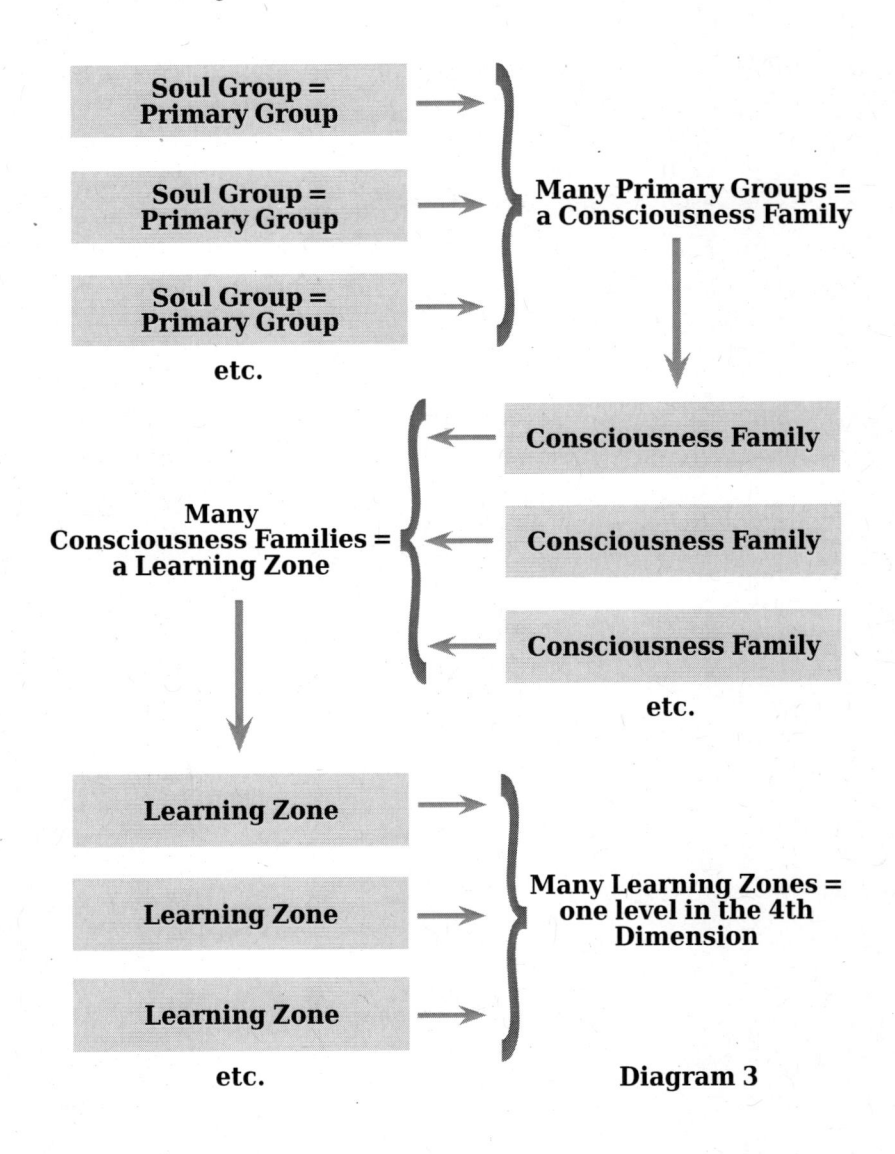

Soul Group = Primary Group →   } **Many Primary Groups = a Consciousness Family**

Soul Group = Primary Group →

etc.

↓

Many Consciousness Families = a Learning Zone { ← **Consciousness Family**

← **Consciousness Family**

← **Consciousness Family**

etc.

↓

Learning Zone →

Learning Zone →   } **Many Learning Zones = one level in the 4th Dimension**

Learning Zone →

etc.

Diagram 3

Eleven

Coming Home

The fourth dimension, called the astral world (see diagram 2), mirrors something that is not ultimate, pure reality, just as life on earth is not the ultimate reality. Pure soul essence shines through the astral form's vibrations, which are finer than earth vibrations. Ultimate reality is purest consciousness, purest conscious love, which encompasses not only the fourth dimension but every dimension that exists, including the nine that we as humans can experience.

Advanced awareness is only found beyond all form and duality. Mistakes, preconceptions, and conflicts come into being only through different kinds of form. Pure, divine awareness is, however, formless, stemming from formless essence. Form is nothing other than distraction and delay, which strengthen the illusion of limited time and space. The soul is eternally endless. It is a beam from the heart of the divine, clothed in a form or, when advanced in its evolution, also unclothed. The clothing can change, but the content cannot.

After the soul has passed through the transitional zone, it arrives in its soul group, or primary group (see Diagram 3). Here its journey ends for a while. It has come home to trusted friends and partners. The soul group is a unity of beings who are in intensive contact with each other, just as is normally the case with families on earth. Members of the group have a deep and encompassing sensitivity for one another. Everyone knows everything about everyone else. They treat each other with much humor and kindness, and learn and reflect together about their lives on earth. Learning is joyful, stimulating, and always by free choice. The primary group is the soul's provisional home, and sometimes for a longer period of time, provided the soul hasn't isolated itself on the way home. If, however, its consciousness is well advanced in its evolution, it may hurry through the astral world like a lightning flash in order to live its love in a higher dimension. All the soul beings in the primary group have a similar level of consciousness and stay together most of the time, though at any time a soul may contact another group if it wishes to or if that would help its evolution. I call this a secondary group.

Diary Entry

Guide: "You have come to your soul group. What will you do now?"

Gerhard: "I am so happy to be home. I'm overwhelmed with joy to see my close relatives again."

Guide: "Do you still think about earth, about the physical world?"

Gerhard: "It seems to be very far away, as in a fog. My life there was not pleasant. I felt isolated and misunderstood."

Guide: "What are you doing now with your friends?"

Gerhard: "I'll tell them about what I experienced there. It's like coming to the end of an unpleasant journey."

Guide: "May I ask you and your friends some questions? It would make me very happy if you would permit it."

Gerhard: "Yes, but first I want to ask Oni, the group teacher."

Oni and five soul friends from the primary group join us and we form a circle. Everyone is friendly and welcoming. I feel accepted and respected.

Guide: "What is the main thing your group does?"

Katja: "We all go to school. We study either together or in separate places."

Guide: "Do you mean that you go to the spiritual school center?"

Katja: "Yes; for example, to the libraries. There we read our life books and sometimes talk to each other about them. We draw analyses from our physical lives. We can see how certain segments of our lives would have been different if we had made other choices in particular situations. It's not judgmental, and is very absorbing."

Guide: "Can you be a bit more precise?"

Katja: "Yes. We watch a past life on earth like a theatrical play. We acted in it, and now we observe ourselves to see how we played our roles."

Marion: "I, for example, didn't play my role well. I really wanted to practice devotion and charity. At first I was totally convinced that it is very easy to be one hundred percent there for others, for my loved ones. I had five children, but I always had the feeling that I was coming up short, that nothing was left for me. I felt that I couldn't develop myself, was very often discontented, and forgot my real task and role. I made my life difficult. When I came back here, everyone laughed at me and teased me. Now even I have to laugh. It is quite amusing how seriously we take everything on earth and how we miss the important things."

Guide: "How did you know what your task was on earth?"

Marion: "One doesn't know. Circumstances show you, and deep in your heart you sense it. Your theater role is deeply imprinted within your being, but circumstances often hinder you from looking in the right spot inside."

Guide: "Can you tell me again the purpose of studying life's books in the library atmosphere?"

Sascha: "We help each other go through our mistakes and discover that mistakes can also stimulate our growth. Our teacher helps us when we get stuck. We discuss a lot in order to gain a different point of view."

Guide: *"Are there other libraries or learning centers you can also visit?"*

Hermann: *"There are centers where we learn to transfer energy. We learn how to create forms, how to dissolve them, and how to change them. There is another school — it is called the harmonizing school."*

Guide: *"What does one learn there?"*

Hermann: *"We harmonize and balance disturbed energy. When a soul comes here with energy that is ill and unbalanced, the first thing is to work on balancing it. We learn what to look for and how to do this. There are huge differences. When we have become good harmonizers, sometimes we are given tasks in the transition zone or the healing center, which are separated from each other."*

Guide: *"Who comes here with disturbed energy?"*

Josef, who had been very quiet and reserved: *"Beings who were very fearful or who were in wars, beings who were tortured or experienced a terrible death."*

Guide: *"Are you one of the souls who is a trained harmonizer?"*

Josef: *"On earth I was a doctor and completely engrossed in science. I wanted to fix everything. Now I have learned the method of harmonizing. It has expanded me immensely."*

Guide: *"How does one harmonize?"*

Josef: "By building forms with light, sounds, and colors. We play with rays of light, weave them, twirl them and stretch them out, dissolve them and connect them. First we watch our teachers do this for quite a while and then we do it ourselves. It requires some finesse. My whole group is happy when I make progress. Now I am often at the healing center and help there. Sometimes I go to the transition zone. There are also confused souls there whom I help when necessary, but that isn't easy, because we may never force anyone."

Twelve

The Astral World

It isn't easy to describe the way of life or circumstances in the fourth dimension. While on the one hand it can be compared to conditions on earth, on the other hand, the differences are enormous. The most obvious difference is the finer grade of substances and, at times, quickly changing forms. The glory of the colors is far more transparent and glowing. Depending on the level, streams of thoughts of various qualities continually move through the atmosphere. The outer border of the astral world reaches almost to the moon's sphere of influence. The lowest zone is near the earth or directly on the earth's surface, but is normally invisible to the physical eye. The moon and the earth, depending on their positions, are between 221,000 and 253,000 miles apart. There are seven levels in this zone, with differing degrees of density that can be roughly divided into three groupings:

» The seventh, the lowest, is very dense;

» the sixth, fifth, and fourth are the middle levels;

» the third, second, and first are the upper levels.

Just like here on earth in the third dimension, where there are differences in the density of solids, liquids, and gases, so there are also differences in densities in the astral world. The astral substances have seven degrees of density that, in turn, can be sorted into seven levels, which can penetrate each other. The seventh level is like a coarse substance: it is very dense and somewhat narrow, and darkness is often seen.

THE ASTRAL BODY

Besides the physical body and the etheric body around it, human beings also have an astral body, which is made up of subatomic particles. The astral body, which when seen through clairvoyant eyes is similar to the physical body, is the carrier of feelings. Although all humans have an astral body, very few are actually fully aware of its existence. Aborigines call it *the double.*

In order to understand the life that a person enters into after the physical body has died, it is helpful to understand the nature of the astral body as well as its possibilities and limitations. Only then can one develop a comprehensive understanding for the entire nature of human beings, for even the astral body is not the end of our awareness. Our existence as humans consists of many dimensions. The astral body is a four-dimensional carrier of consciousness, which manifests its life mainly in this fourth dimension.

The sixth, fifth, and fourth levels have a similar quality of life to that on earth, but in a finer condition. Some of the beings here tend to establish themselves more permanently, because life here is much more vital and has a joyful force flowing through it. The finer body reacts quickly to thoughts and feelings. There is no place to hide, no masks — everyone instantly senses the feelings of others. Every emotion visibly glows and pulses through the soul being, radiating in innumerable characteristic colors.

Although the third, second, and first levels occupy almost the same space, one senses that the soul beings are far removed from the earthly sphere. Here one finds beautiful, spectacularly luminous, splendidly colorful schools, houses, and landscapes that are far more magnificent than anything on earth. All here share uplifting, happy energy and trust, so that some souls think they have arrived in paradise.

In the fourth dimension the soul lives similarly to existence on the physical plane, but is lighter and more transparent. Because of its astral structure, it cannot be destroyed or injured. Atmospheric or climatic conditions cannot affect it. Sleep is unnecessary, and there is no aging process as with a physical body. With some practice, the soul can rapidly alter the form by the sheer force of will. Astral vision reveals a completely different color spectrum beyond the scope of colors that are visible on earth. Infrared and ultraviolet rays are clearly recognizable, and all the colors shine with wonderful transparency. Life energy (prana/ether) is visible, as are thought waves and forms. There are no shadows. Objects are seen simultaneously from all sides. For example, a cupboard would be seen from the front, back, top, bottom, and the inside all at once.

Diary Entry

Guide: "You have arrived in your soul group. How do you feel?"

Norma: "I feel so connected. We have known each other forever. There is great trust, great love."

Guide: "How do you see your friends? Look around you. How would you describe the way they look?"

Norma: "Why do you ask me? You see them yourself."

Guide: "Yes, but I would like to hear from you what you see."

Norma: "I see them like on earth, only with more light around each one. We are all shimmering brightly and can change ourselves. Each of my friends has a specific field of light zooming around him, like fireflies. Everyone has his own primary pattern in different intensities of color."

Guide: "Look farther away. How do the other soul beings appear to you?"

Norma: "In the distance I see different fields of light that are moving. As I go nearer they are becoming visible forms, human forms. I've learned that light energy particles move around us either more slowly or rapidly. When a soul can send the light out quickly, then they create shades of blue and violet. Souls that are advanced can play with their light particles."

Guide: "What does it feel like when you hug one of your friends?"

Norma: "Like this!" Norma takes my face in both her hands, gives me a tender kiss, and strokes my head. "When our friends come back to our soul family, we greet each one individually, but we always surround each one with our personal energy like a gentle caress. It is our welcoming ceremony."

Guide: "Do you always stay together in your soul group?"

Norma: "No, there are certain phases during which I don't remain with my soul group but go to other learning levels, like to the place for transformation or to the music center. All these places promote my development; however, we always come back to our soul group and exchange experiences."

It is impossible to describe impressions in this dimension, the homeland sphere. The light is so much more intense than on earth. It shines through everything, and everything is bathed in light. The beauty of the trees, the flowers, fields, and houses is overwhelming, and the sight of human beings is invigorating and uplifting. Here there is a truly different and infinitely more complex way of life.

Human bodies are bathed in softly shimmering, gloriously flowing robes that correspond exactly to their life frequencies. A wonderful weightlessness and elasticity allow the soul to quickly forget the heaviness of the physical body. The wish to move arises immediately. Every thought and every feeling pulsates through the soul, often visibly.

Enhanced consciousness and a better ability to adapt are expressions of the new quality of life. The outer form becomes much more in tune with the inner being and is independent of earthly rhythms. The myriad colors, which are at one and the same time sounds, reflect individual patterns of movement and the characteristics of a soul group or of an individual soul being. Light energy, vibrational forms, wave movements, and sound vibrations allow one to recognize different members of a soul group. In this sphere, tones have a much greater power of expression than we know of here on earth. The names of beings can be compared to musical chords that harbor their own hidden meanings.

Diary Entry

Guide: "What is your name here in the spiritual world?"

Spirit being: "My name is Arondo."

Guide: "If you had to describe yourself, what would you say about your appearance?"

Arondo: "I experience myself as living light that is music at the same time."

Guide: "What exactly is the color of your light? Can you distinguish it?"

Arondo: "In my light there are traces of gold and violet, but actually my being sends out tones that are rhythmical and sometimes melodious. It is the quality of my spiritual ability to express myself. I am heard and seen."

Guide: "Is it possible for you to change your color and sound, perhaps through your thoughts?"

Arondo: "Yes, I can change it, but the way I am now shows the exact level of my development. So the color and sound are relatively stable. If you live here, there is a way of learning that is universal, but we decide on the framework ourselves. To change ourselves, we create differing light and tone qualities and different movements as we create new forms. Our leader and teacher supports us in this for there are different realities, differing spaces, differing clothing, differing ways in which our light-robes work. All of it must always be in harmony with our essential soul energy."

Guide: "Thank you, Arondo. That has helped me."

Thirteen

The Death of a Child

From our earthly point of view, the death of a child is an endlessly painful experience for parents and relatives. A child lives not only in the parents' home, but also in their hearts, and when the child dies, it is as though the parents lose their own lives. This causes a painful fissure in their emotional world, and their own lives seem to fall apart. Occasionally in my practice I have experienced that parents, even years later, still had not recovered emotionally. If one has never lost a child, the suffering that parents go through and the emotional wounds they carry are unimaginable. If, however, we view the death of a small child from a spiritual and otherworldly point of view and wish to understand, we must learn to regard it differently.

Our lives and thinking in the 20th and 21st centuries, particularly in Western society, are so fixated on image, on the physical body and material things, that our cultural fences limit our ability to perceive. We no longer recognize a child as a multidimensional being. We don't see it as a soul being that has entered into a partnership with a physical body here on earth.

Young children are still flush with the purity of their own souls. That is why every openhearted person is moved by the healing and loving purity of these little ones. Is it not so that in the eyes of children we catch glimpses of eternity? Don't we sense their great wisdom, if our vision has not been distorted through one-sided logical and analytical thinking? Sublime angels around every child help its soul to connect more deeply with the growing physical body. Children are imbued with the breath of the loving God (divine). They are tender blossoms filled with the light of eternal love. Each of their faces is the face of an angel whose spiritual presence is rarely recognized by the clouded eyes of grownups.

When a small child loses its earthly life, its soul being is not dead, of course. It has merely laid aside its physical clothing. Why does the child want to leave us so soon? The child's soul eyes come from a higher dimension, and they see angels ascending and descending. Even after birth, when the soul is merged with the physical body, the child is still deeply bonded with the other world. From the perspective of a higher dimension, life here on earth takes shape differently than we believe. The child's soul can have impressions that are quite unlike those of its parents who identify themselves entirely with their physical bodies. In its development the soul of a child can, for example, be much more mature than those of its parents. When a child is born and brings healing energy from the other side, it can help its parents lead their lives with deeper consciousness and knowledge.

~ Witness Report ~

Gert: "The meeting was in the hospital. Our son, David, who was born much too early and under difficult circumstances, lay in the incubator. He was so small and frail that he fit in the palm of my hand. He did not want to stay long in this world. What task did he have to fulfill? One day before his departure, what we call death, we were with him — as we were every day — and as always he had his eyes closed and was asleep. But suddenly, as I spoke to him, he opened his eyes for a moment — a moment far too short to measure, but longer than eternity, or so it seemed to me. This glance was so deep and so strong that I will never forget it. Today, after all these years, I still feel it like a laser beam that penetrated everything and was as deep as the universe. Back then I said to him, "Look, your mother is here." Miraculously, he turned his head to Elizabeth who was standing on the other side of the incubator and looked at her."

Elizabeth: "His bright eyes went right to my heart. Time stood still, and for that moment I felt that I was beyond space and time, flooded with happiness and light. This telepathic communication that I perceived filled me completely and was too great

to describe. His look seemed like a dream, and was for us a greeting and a goodbye at the same time.
One day later David left this world."

— Gert and Elizabeth in Stuttgart

For those who feel that the death of a child is premature, the following considerations may be helpful. The child died:

» because the soul being had the task of helping its parents by creating an opening for them, through pain, to learn to view the world from a different perspective;

» because the partnership between the physical body and the soul with their differing vibrations weren't matched well enough and the soul didn't "fit" the body;

» because an early death was desired by the soul and was necessary for its development.

Witness Report

"I was overwhelmed with grief after Grisha's death, but I did notice in the following seven days, that there was something else besides the numbing shock. I felt something between openness and pain. I felt that a part of me was still strongly bound to the child, as if I were accompanying him on a journey, but I couldn't explain it.

"Grisha didn't die at home, but at my parents' house, and only later was brought to the hospital where my husband and I held the wake at his bedside. The idea of returning home without him was unbearable to me. As I climbed the stairs, I was sick with pain. Suddenly it struck me, *I need some pain pills and tranquilizers.*

"But just as quickly I thought, *Get through it, pills are an escape. Perhaps there is sense and reason behind all pain and suffering, a bright spot.* Then I opened the door to my apartment.

"What I experienced then is impossible to describe. The apartment in which Grisha had lived with us seemed full of light and scent. Suddenly I knew that Grisha was there and was waiting for me. I felt his presence and was deeply touched and comforted. The unusual scent throughout the apartment was like a brilliant, pure, uplifting powder. This scent dominated and covered everything there. I knew in that moment that Grisha didn't want us to be sad and that it was important for him that my husband and I didn't get stuck in pain and suffering, because it could hinder our own development. For exactly seven days I experienced this refined light and scent in our house intensely. In the three years that followed I always experienced the same light and scent on the anniversary of Grisha's death and on his birthday.

"I recognize how important a year of mourning is. I've changed as I have gone through the four seasons and through the festivities. I also noticed that death has many similarities with birth. The first year of a child's life, with its discoveries and transitions, is for me like the first year of mourning after the child's death. There is so much to experience until the seemingly everyday life comes to the forefront once more. Just as the birth, so also the death of a child changes one's perceptions and consciousness enormously — especially when one has developed confidence to face pain and not numb oneself, because therein also lies transformation and salvation.

"Birth and death are similar. With birth I must go through pain, I must surrender to the pains of giving birth in order to experience the deep joy of the new in its entirety. The great miracle that I was allowed to experience through the death of my son is the absolute sureness that there is no death, only transformation."

—Martina from Hamlin

Fourteen

The Wake

The wake is especially meaningful for those who have just died (and are newly born into the spiritual world). It used to be common for the body to be kept at home in an open casket surrounded with flowers. At least one candle was left burning, and prayers were offered to ease the transition and to help take leave in peace. I believe many of us don't realize that we may keep the dead with us for a while at home. Even if someone dies in the hospital or in an eldercare facility, the relatives may take the body home. There are, however, some hospitals, funeral parlors,[14] and elder homes that now have beautiful, quiet rooms where one can take leave in a dignified way.

If a beloved person dies when he or she is quite old, it is of course sad, but even so, in a certain way nature's order is showing its effect on human nature. It is different and much more difficult for those left behind to accept it when:

» a young child departs from the family;

- » someone dies violently in an accident;
- » a person has been killed (murder, manslaughter, war, execution);
- » an ill or despairing person chooses suicide.

In every case it is an act of love to hold a wake. Even when the body is not in the home, a wake can still be held and is always an act of love. Love is a natural radiance that crosses the borders between dimensions. Through our love we are deeply connected beyond death.

How to Hold a Wake

The deceased lies in a coffin in front of you. Be sure that there are flowers in the room, for the fine and high vibrations from blossoms make the ethereal curtain between the dimensions more transparent. At least one candle should be burning, preferably orange in color, because this light loosens the ether. Small, red memorial candles may also be used. Now sit comfortably on a chair. Have soft music playing, if possible. Close your eyes and imagine that you are standing in front of a curtain, which is slowly opening. You enter into a wonderful landscape. Behind you the curtain closes. Here in this new landscape you seek a spot where you feel safe and secure. Now ask a clear and definite question of the dead person.

It might happen that the soul of the dead person will appear before you, but don't expect it. You will receive an answer or a sign. Trust your first impression — it is your answer. Allow yourself plenty of time. The moment will come when you are certain, "Now it is good." Then go back to the curtain, close it behind you, and say, "I let you go, my loved one, my beloved [NAME], I bless you with the power of my love." Open your eyes and say a prayer.

Many times I have met dead ones who have been reborn into the next finer level. Again and again I sensed similar reactions, which I summarize in the following four points:

» The dead (newly born), independent of the cause of their death, are absolutely certain that their death occurred at the right moment, with the exception of those who chose suicide (see the chapter "The Bewildered Soul").

» They are filled with deep gratitude when loved ones were with them in their last hours and a wake was held.

» They have a strong wish for those left behind to realize that they are not dead. They know now that there is no death — only a transformation — and that they live on in their soul being.

» They wish that those who are left behind in sorrow return to life and not remain stuck in pain.

Witness Report

"During her long period of chemotherapy, Stephanie was extremely patient and always thoughtful in finding ways to create joyful moments for her friends and family. For example, she only agreed to undergo chemotherapy after her friends agreed to let her buy them something 'in return.' One time, when my wife, Maria, was with her, she bought a marzipan candy bar from her pocket money, because she knew her mother liked it so much.

"After Stephanie had a relapse, her parents decided that they wouldn't ask Stephanie to undergo any more chemotherapy. Stephanie lived for one more year in the circle of her family before she died. During this time she was unusually happy and unconcerned — in fact she even went to school.

"The final phase of her physical life lasted a week or two, during which she lay in her darkened bedroom. When her mother was told that the end was nearing, she asked a priest to baptize Stephanie and her sister Vaneros. Maria and I were asked to be godparents, and I accompanied this moving ceremony on my guitar. Weak as she was, Stephanie let everything glide over her. At the end of the ceremony, while we sang the song *Let us praise and thank the Lord all together,* to our surprise, Stephanie sat up in bed and sang loudly with us. After that she sank back into her pillows.

"Following the ceremony, we were sitting with her parents in the dining room. Suddenly, Stephanie was standing there and wanted to eat with us. We were astonished and believed a miracle was taking place. One hour later, however, Stephanie was lying limply once again in her bed. On the 8th of December, the Day of the Immaculate Conception, Stephanie died quietly and in peace.

—Claus from Heidelberg

In my diary entries I found a dialogue with Melanie, who had also died of leukemia. I include this dialogue here because Stephanie's transition could have happened in a similar way.

Diary Entry

As Melanie awakes from behind the veil, she is surrounded by soul helpers who will prepare her for her new life in the healing center.

Melanie: "Where am I? Do I have to have chemotherapy again?"

Ornando (a helper from the healing center): "My dear little one, you are here in a recovery home. You are healthy, Melanie, completely healthy."

Melanie: "No, I will never be healthy again. My mother says that I have leukemia. I am going to go to God and Maria, the heavenly Mother. Where is my mother?"

Guide: "When you get up and feel how strong you are, then you can go to your mother. Come, let me show you how strong you are. Now, get up, Melanie."

Melanie: "You are all so kind, but I am very weak, don't you know that?"

The guide takes Melanie carefully in his arms and helps her get out of bed. Melanie is surprised at how securely she can stand on her feet. Smiling, she looks at Ornando and the guide.

Melanie: "Has a miracle happened to me? Did God perform a miracle?"

Ornando: "Yes, a miracle has happened, that's one way of putting it."

Overwhelmed with joy, Stephanie takes a few steps forward, turns around in circles, raises her arms, runs to Ornando, and flings her arms around him.

Guide: "Come, Melanie, I will show you a wonderful garden full of flowers and butterflies."

Melanie nods her head and slips her hand into that of her guide. When she sees the enchanting garden, she runs from flower to flower, smelling each one, and hugs the trees. She hops and jumps with happiness, and rejoices and sings. Then she chases after the butterflies.

Melanie: "Now let's go to my mama. She will be so happy to see that I am healthy again."

Ornando: "Yes, we will go to your mama now, but it will be a little different from what you expect, my dear little angel. You will be able to see your mama, but she won't be able to recognize you, because you are now in a different sphere."

Melanie looks at Orlando with big eyes and becomes very quiet. She seems to be becoming aware of something.

Melanie: "Have I died?"

Ornando: "You are now here in your soul body. Your physical body is a vessel for your soul that you live in for a short time. Then, at some point, the soul leaves this vessel and comes to its true home. Your vessel, dearest Melanie, was ill and weak, and then you left it. There is no death for the soul, Melanie."

Melanie: "Then am I in heaven. Is this heaven here?"

Ornando: "Not the heaven that you are thinking of. But you see that it is very, very beautiful here."

Melanie: "Then where are Jesus and Mary and the angels?"

Ornando: "They will come to you soon, Melanie, but you are not yet prepared enough for their infinite brilliance, for their penetrating light. Just wait a little, for you will surely meet them."

Melanie is quiet for a while, and one senses that she is lost in thought.

Melanie: "I understand. I am alive, although I am dead. Only my physical body is dead. I really want to go to my mama."

Ornando: "We will try, Melanie. It won't be easy, because your mother is very sad, but we will try."

Melanie: "How do we get to her?"

Ornando: "We have to picture your mama and then you have to love her very much. That is how you create heavenly streams and waves that you can travel on like a road. Your soul must be sensitive, like a pointer on a measuring instrument; then you can go through your love to wherever you want to be. If your mama is alert to your vibrations, she will feel your presence."

Melanie quickly understands how she can reach her mother.

Melanie: "I can see my mother." (Melanie whoops for joy.) "I think she knows I am here. ... I am trying to tell her that I am healthy again. I am sure that inside she feels it. ... Ornando, I told her that I am in everlasting life, in another sphere."

Ornando: "My dear, we are always in everlasting life, even when we are on earth. At the beginning of our development, our eyes can only see the created things, the forms. But seeing only the forms is not enough; humans must learn to see behind things. With their sight they must learn to see the higher value in things. Then the human opens himself a thousandfold and recognizes that his soul lives from experience to experience. Life on earth is an experience. Death is *an experience. The different spheres are an experience. We will gather many, many experiences."*

Melanie: "Do you also mean the experience of where Jesus and Mary are?"

Ornando: "Yes."

Fifteen

The Schooling Centers

After physical death, every person goes to the place appropriate for his consciousness. There he meets trusted friends and family members with whom he voluntarily attends schooling centers when he isn't spending time studying alone. There, creativity in all possible forms and types are taught and encouraged. These serve to further develop the soul. There are centers for music, art, dance, architecture, ethical use of speech, healing, willpower training, philosophy, galactic travel, and much more.

On earth many people believe that at the moment of death they instantly rise to be with God, or that Jesus and Mary will stand before them to receive them. They also believe that on the other side they will reign over perfect knowledge and will instantly understand and grasp all spirituality. That isn't so. Life on the other side — at first in the fourth dimension — is similar to life on earth. Only in the higher dimensions does it gradually change. Ideas about the "other side" are always right — yet at the same time inaccurate. Every idea that is posited and held as dogma represents a false approach. We should be aware that our idea of "heaven" is always what we long for while here on earth. We overlook what the spiritual world actually is: unlimited diversity.

Imagine that you had never before been on this planet and have to tell someone who also has never been here about your travels. It would be practically impossible to fully explain and include all the details. There are wonderful, fantastic buildings, superb architectural achievements, but also derelict shacks. There is a luxuriant, almost unfathomable diversity of flora, but also nearly lifeless deserts, black fields of lava, and inaccessible mountain ranges. Also there are innumerable animal species, more than one could ever see in one lifetime. On our planet people live on varied social levels, and are of differing races, colors, and sizes. Humans live together, but never get to know everyone. There are health resorts, but also places to be avoided because they are life threatening. There are oceans teeming with myriad underwater worlds, and areas of eternal ice as well.

If one were to isolate one aspect of this diversity and claim it, and nothing else, to be what the planet earth is like, that picture would be completely false. It is the same with the fourth dimension, the lowest, densest sphere on the other side. The diversity is prodigiously great, and all life is related very closely to that here on earth. What I am sharing here from my experiences and perceptions is only a tiny section of the endlessly diverse, multifaceted levels of being.

Diary Entry

"What beauty I experienced today! Never have I seen such a blaze of colors here on earth. It was as if light were lying on everything — or perhaps, better still, light was streaming out of everything alive. Fine points of light danced around every blade of grass, the trees, and the flowers like delicate golden kernels. At the same time, the light illuminated everything from the inside out. I held my breath in deep happiness and peace at this wondrous beauty. A marvelous scent poured out of all living things. I experienced complete oneness in God; I felt myself surrounded by divine love. All life was intrinsically being in God, and the light I perceived didn't stream from above or below or sideways, but rather glowed through all things. Trees, flowers, and blades of grass were bathed in a gentle luster of penetrating splendor and glory. For the first time I understood what it means to 'live in God.' In church services I had so often heard the words 'through Him, with Him, and in Him.' Though I had repeated them, I had never experienced what it really means to live in Him. We are always living in God, but in the higher spheres we are more conscious, it is clearer to us. There we can experience godly light directly."

≈

We are always ourselves
We cannot escape our wholeness.
Divinity is far more than life and death.
That is why in the universe there is far more to experience
Than we imagine.
The show of perception continues eternally.
God is neither here nor there.
God is the source of all being, is here, always here,
Penetrating consciousness in all that is.

≈

Diary Entry

We are standing in front of a large, circular building surrounded by arcades, a schooling center with a golden dome.

Guide: "Where are we here?"

Jenny: "This is my schooling center, which has a big library attached."

Guide: "Does anyone tell you to go to school?"

Jenny: "Of course not. It is free choice and so interesting. I am happy to learn here."

Guide: "Are there other schooling centers that you can go to?"

Jenny: "Yes, but at the moment I want to be together with my friends and my teacher, Baldi. We are very close and have wonderful discussions about what we are studying."

Guide: "Are there different levels of knowledge amongst you?"

Jenny: "Yes. Of course, those who can implement what they have learned, and also love more, are more advanced."

Guide: "Can you tell me what you and friends do in the library and at the schooling center?"

Jenny: "Come with me and I'll show you. Let's go to the library first and look at the books."

Guide: "What kinds of books are these?"

Jenny: "These are the life books from all of us. Additionally, there are science books about other systems, worlds, books about ethics, game books, and religious books."

Guide: "What is inside the life books?"

Jenny: "When we open them, they show us living, moving pictures, like television on earth. Here is my life book. When I open it I see small excerpts from my life, as well as the opportunities that I didn't take. Look here: I had no sense of humor, and I took everything very personally. Here in this part I am very crabby. Unfortunately, this trait stuck with me during my whole earthly life. When I look at this aspect of my life, I am saddened and shake my head at myself. These books are intended to allow us to focus on our past deeds in order to learn from them. My friends help me with it, and I help them."

Guide: "Can you tell me what the lessons are like?"

Jenny: "In the dance lesson we meld with the music. You must know that the tones are alive and that we ourselves become sounds. We transform ourselves through movement into tones. We create light and sound patterns through our movements. Sometimes we all laugh, because we don't understand the tones, and the light-tone patterns lose their harmony. Then my teacher, Baldi, helps me to work out the difference between hearing the tones and becoming one with them. Baldi is wonderful and has a lot of patience with us."

Guide: "Does she also teach lessons in humor?"

Jenny: "Humor and discipline belong together. Yes, Baldi is an outstanding teacher."

Guide: "Does Baldi always stay with you and your friends?"

Jenny: "Baldi comes and goes, but I am always together with my friends. We discuss a lot about our lessons."

Guide: "When you look at your earthly life in your life book, what about it makes you sad?"

Jenny: "That I had such a lack of self-discipline and humor. I could have been more serene. But now I am."

Guide: "Can you say what made you happy?"

Jenny: "Yes, whenever I was allowed to sit on my father's lap. That was heaven for me."

Diary Entry

I (the guide) am standing outdoors in nature, in front of a group of soul beings, surrounded by trees and unusually beautiful, very tall flowers. Everything here seems to be light blue. Not that the trees and flowers are light blue, no, they are brightly colored, but everywhere there is a sheen of light blue, whereas in other places it was light green or pale violet or slightly golden. Sometimes in autumn on earth, at certain times of day, the sun seems to cover everything in a golden glow. That can give you an idea of what it is like.

Guide: "May I join you to ask some questions?"

Helena: "But of course. We already knew that you were coming. You are welcome here."

Guide: "Why is everything here transparent light blue and in other places pale violet?"

Helena: "All light comes from the source. Here in this spot we are very connected to the source, the genesis of all being. Each sphere has its own shade of color. Not everyone can endure the great intensity of all the light vibrations, and so only those souls who feel good in this place come here. You might say that some soul beings feel drained by the high frequencies, as if they were disintegrating or fading away. That is why each being lingers only where it feels good. The transparent colors indicate a higher frequency, a higher vibration in the specific sphere where one lives. The more you are connected to the source, the more transparent you appear. But you always remain your own being, only with other shades."

Guide: "Is the source God?"

Helena: "God is both impersonal and personal. The source that penetrates everything is the impersonal part of God. The source is the unnamable eternal, which penetrates everything. It is the essence of all being. It is the unconditional love in which we live. Jesus Christ was the perfect representative of the source. He called the source Father."

Guide: "Is it possible for me to meet Jesus?"

Helena: "Yes, of course, but it is always a gift and not a given. Jesus lives in levels that extend far above us. Nonetheless, we can be bonded with Him."

Guide: "Do I have to call Jesus? And what preconditions are necessary for him to come?"

Helena: "You recognize that you are bonded with him through stillness and inward listening. If you call him with true love and open yourself to this immensity, he might appear to you. He is so wise, so full of light and love, that his presence always begets devotion. He helps us to unite more deeply with the source and to expand our consciousness more and more until we are completely open and entirely one with the source, the Father."

Guide: "What is your task here, Helena? Is this also a place of learning?"

Helena: "Yes, I'm here with the majority of my soul group to learn and perfect myself. We are learning to transmit very high thought energy and to send it so adroitly that it doesn't decompose. Besides that, we are learning to receive thought signals and calls for help."

Guide: "Can you explain that more exactly? How can thought energy decompose?"

Helena: "It depends on who the receiver is. It is very easy with my friends, but we practice often in the transitional zone or sometimes also with our teacher, Faro, in the denser earth zone. Our thought energy has to be so clear and precise that it can prevail over negative human emotions. For example, if we receive a call for help from a person who is in an emotional crisis, is filled with fear, or is suffering great pain, he is also unconsciously sending out a lot of negative energy, which we sense. There are some souls whom we are taking care of and whose soul frequencies we know. We can receive this soul energy when we consciously tune ourselves in to it."

Guide: "Then are you also a soul helper, Helena?"

Helena: "Yes, but this work is preparing me for something else."

Guide: "Please describe what it is that you do exactly in order to help these people."

Helena: "I plant thoughts and feelings of peace and hope. At first, I create in myself an absolutely clear and harmonious thought field of the crystalline substances of peace and love — a transparent, strongly resonating field of peace energy and new inspirational impulses. I whisper something in their ears or in their hearts, I sing above their heads, and wrap them with tenderness until I have guided them in another direction."

Guide: "Isn't that a guardian angel's work?"

Helena: "There are many workers in God's vineyard. Some soul beings can hardly be reached because they are stuck in tribulation and fear or because they are too distracted and scatterbrained. Many human souls are so dulled that it requires artful skill to reach them. Our holy guardian angels have a high, pure vibration, and we help them with getting the connection between angel and human being to function again. We prepare the way, so to speak. It is important that we adhere to the law never to impose anything. Everyone must work on his own problems. Faro, our teacher, is wonderful. He always knows exactly when one can intervene and when not to."

Guide: "What is your biggest problem when you are working with people in the earth zone?"

Helena: "Fear and absentmindedness."

Guide: "Which people are the easiest?"

Helena: "Those who are open, inwardly calm, and composed."

Sixteen

Soul Guides and Angels

Many dying people are met by relatives or friends who have died before them, so that during the transition a feeling of trust and protection is established. Sometimes a soul is received by his spiritual teachers, his soul guide, or his guardian angel. These are beings full of warm, loving, and uplifting energy who, through constant impulses, help the soul become conscious of the continuity of all life.

The soul guides are teachers who encourage the development and expansion of consciousness. They are harmonizers, healers, researchers, protectors, and guardians in many respects. The spiritual maturity of a soul guide determines whether he only works with one charge or several. It is always the responsibility of advanced soul guides to lead to the knowledge of oneness with God. In every soul group, whether the number is large or small, there is a teacher soul at work. Soul guides always have deep compassion for those they are responsible for. However, the way they instruct and educate varies greatly. Our soul guides help us in the earth sphere, assisting us even when we don't see them. They support us when we are crossing the threshold so that we can better lay aside our physical bodies as we pass through the transitional zone. A good soul guide always endeavors to be sensitive and induce positive change so that a soul awakens conscious of its real freedom in God. In supporting a soul, its maturity is naturally an important factor. Angels ring out and radiate the love of God into the sometimes cold hearts of people. Their goodness nourishes the souls. Just as air above a hot fire is warmed, so the angels create warm vortexes of love that nourish souls. If we have already formed a loving contact with our personal guardian angels while on earth, it is possible that during our transition these sublime beings will escort us to another dimension. While we are living here on earth, they already help us through their loving warmth to become lighter and purer. Unfortunately, we often lack the "antennae" to notice their effect. When we have our "heavenly weight" and have left behind all heaviness, earthly attachments, and disharmony, then we may receive a gift — angels will surround us with unconditional love and lead us to our true heavenly home.

Dairy Entry

Guide: "You are the soul guide in your group, Marius. May I ask you some questions?"

Marius: "Yes, you may."

Guide: "What exactly is your task?"

Marius: "I encourage souls to know their true essence."

Guide: "Can you talk a bit about your work?"

Marius: "I am a teaching soul, and I stimulate my soul group so that each of them recognizes the limitlessness of joy and love. I myself am full of joy and poetry. How can I help you to understand the splendor of life? The afterlife, as you call it, knows no boundaries. The planet earth, in comparison, is full of limitations. Understanding on earth does not extend beyond certain circles, whereas here the horizons are endless. Our time here is not like the time of people on earth. Here we travel on 'streets' (beams) of consciousness, and work with heavenly arithmetic that is incomprehensible on earth. Here we are completely free of all greed. It is my task to let every soul under my care resound with the voices of perfect harmony and to hear the song of countless pure tones with their effervescent internal echoes. The soul beings learn to strip themselves layer by layer in order to ignite their core, so that the fire of God's love begins to glow in each one. I teach how to give oneself up to the heavenly streams and to float in them like a leaf in flowing water."

Guide: "So you teach the truth of God's love?"

Marius: "You can't teach truth. The truth doesn't need to be proven, it is fulfilled and revealed. The love of God is not learned; one lives in it and experiences it when the commotion of life is silenced."

Guide: "Marius, in your presence one feels uplifting peace and great trust. It is so easy to open oneself to you."

Marius: "Silence is necessary for a soul to open itself. When you approach a small bird, you must tread softly and be very quiet, lest it lose its trust. The tiniest noise can scare it and then it is gone. That is how it is with heavenly fluidium (fluidity) — the higher the frequency and the more transparent they are, the more sensitive they are. The smallest disharmony can 'frighten' them and carry them off. The soul is permeated with heavenly fluidium, which withdraws entirely when there is disharmony. Thinking is too cumbersome to conjure up a proper picture of the soul. It is difficult for me to describe how precious it is. You would cheer with joy, if you were to recognize your own soul. Human understanding is still important for you, but it is so simply structured! You wouldn't believe how little it can grasp. Many of those whom I teach are like children that can't read. So I teach them to read, to read the limitless spiritual streams."

Guide: "Marius, you are saying that the physical brain on

earth is too coarse to be able to comprehend the very fine spiritual streams. How does thinking here differ to that in earth's sphere?"

Marius: *"On earth, people have the most developed brains of all living beings. The physical brain organ receives the spiritual. The brain's job is to choose from its total consciousness what is appropriate for the person's development and to discard the inappropriate. It is constantly filtering and sorting things out, adjusting to actual life situations or its thought patterns. The human brain is an organ that selects. The essence of whatever it does is the result of repeated selection that has been going on continuously for millions of years during the earth's evolution. The brain filters out of the total consciousness that which is suitable for life on earth. The pure effect of the higher spirit is discovered only by a few.*

"Here, on the other hand, our whole being is attuned to receiving spirit. We take thought forms into our being and then separate them according to their content. We swim in streams of pure consciousness. Our souls must learn to lighten up, just like fingers must loosen up if they are to play the keys of an instrument. The soul's ability to absorb the pure spirit will become finer and finer. Our being's form consists of countless forms and light patterns that receive and digest without filtering. Therefore we must be very careful which spiritual stream we end up in, because the spiritual stream that we are in always vibrates at its own specific frequency.

When we absorb it as information within us, it the same outside of us. A mutual penetration takes place. You become charged with the waves and rhythms, the sound impulses, and the accompanying tiniest substances. If they are pure and transparent, you are full of joy and light and you possess overwhelming insights.

"When this is not the case, you sink down, become heavy, and get into unfavorable streams. Many bad streams that are heavy and full of fear, hate, and ignorance come from the earth's sphere. The only ones on earth who comprehend heaven are those who carry heaven within them. If one doesn't have a bit of heaven in oneself, it will be very hard at first to get used to conditions in the dimension on the other side."

Guide: "Marius, do you sometimes teach in the earth's sphere?"

Marius: "Only very rarely, and then only with humans who are open for 'heaven.' I plant uplifting thought impulses in them."

Guide: "What impulses are those?"

Marius: "That they should never tire of imbuing everything with prayer and godly purity, for then the angels and archangels can really meet them."

Guide: "To which people on earth do you give thought impulses?"

Marius: "Mostly to those souls who belong to my field of responsibility. Sometimes I discover humans who carry a wonderful 'star' within them, but which is covered by a layer of dust. Then I want to help reveal this hidden treasure so that their being once again radiates in its full glory. But I work only very occasionally on earth, as it is very strenuous."

Guide: "Thank you, Marius."

Seventeen

The Bewildered Soul

In this chapter I want to speak about a very delicate matter: what happens to soul beings who caused extreme pain to other humans while on earth, or who in a destructive, emotionally evil and vicious way ignored the laws of love? What happens to those who ride a huge wave of superficiality and ignorance, refusing all spiritual impulses and living instead a life of hate and greed? Does hell really exist, or purgatory, or a place of most terrible exile?

"The Judgment," a scene painted in the Egyptian *Book of the Dead* about 3,300 years ago, shows a man named Ani who has just died and now finds himself between earth and the spiritual home. He stands next to a scale, and is being judged for his deeds on earth. The god Anubis is weighing the heart of the dead man against a feather, the symbol of Ma'at, the goddess of cosmic order, or "what is right." The heart, not the head, or mental prowess, is weighed. If Ani's heart is as light and pure as the feather, then he can enter into the kingdom of the next world. If, however, his heart is not light enough, but is instead heavy with evil and destruction, then a monster, the great devourer, waits nearby ready to gobble him up.

In the Christian view there is the concept of purgatory, a temporary state of exile for lesser sins, and hell for those who have committed truly evil deeds. Purgatory and hell are places of atonement, isolation, and suffering, where one lands as punishment for leading a sinful life. First of all I want to state emphatically that there is no place of eternal punishment and pain, like a prison one is thrown into, where one is condemned forever. The strictest judge of one's past life is oneself! Our teachers, advisors, and friends continually give us impulses for a new orientation, for assistance, healing, and transformation.

Temporary isolation and segregation occur because the "heart" is too heavy, the vibrations around the soul after death are too coarse, or because the soul's raiment is deformed through disharmonious negativity. The cover appears distorted. Hell and isolation occur because the soul cannot recognize itself like this. Heaviness and extreme attachment to the material prevent clear access to the essential soul light, and allow the soul being to sink into darkness, into zones of disorientation. Human beings who were under bad influences will experience a correction after their deaths, if they want it. As a result, they become more open and receptive, and sooner or later they will be drawn to the light.

What are the decisive criteria that prevent a soul from wanting or being able to return home to its own soul group?

- » Ignorant, loveless behavior on earth creates an attitude and thinking that correspond to vibrations in the ethereal and astral auras, which after death at first attract the same fields that isolate them from higher and finer fields.

- » Through his pronounced immaturity, the dead one has spiritual blockages and exhibits an enormous attachment to particular places or people whom he either hates or, through misunderstood love, cannot release. He remains in the immediate sphere of the living.

- » Physical life on earth seems to have ended too soon through murder, accident, war, or natural catastrophe. This shock can — though it doesn't have to — cause a traumatic experience.

Diary Entry

Guide: "Natalie, you have now arrived in your soul group. From the time of your physical death, how long did it take to get here?"

Natalie: "Time here is different than on earth, and so I can't say exactly, but from the earthly viewpoint it took some time to get rid of my heaviness. My soul guide, Marana, who came to me repeatedly, made it possible. It was as if I were blind, and the distance to the light seemed endless. I was deaf to all the harmonies that called to me from the essence of my soul, and I was mute. It was impossible for me to utter a single word of beauty."

Guide: "What made it so difficult for you, Natalie? Do you want to talk about it?"

Natalie: "I felt awful in my physical body, and I felt enormous hatred for my divorced husband. I did everything I could think of to harm him. After my death and arrival here in this sphere, I couldn't let go of the habit of causing him pain, especially since in the beginning I didn't even realize that I wasn't living physically."

Guide: "Why didn't you realize that you were on a different plane?"

Natalie: "After I came into this sphere, I experienced a kind of coma or unconsciousness, which lasted for some time. Then, there were occasional intervals of hazy, foggy, unreal moments. My hatred was like a branded mark that couldn't be removed. In short, ugly flashbacks it kept coming back. Often, I also had fleeting glimpses of Marana who smiled at me and then disappeared again. As I slowly got better, I could see Marana for longer periods. At first, everything around me was dark, and I had only a shadowy sense of other beings. I was alone and I wanted to be alone."

Guide: "What happened when you became conscious of your situation?"

Natalie: "Marana gave me private lessons, so to speak, so that I learned to differentiate between what had a negative effect on my consciousness and what was beneficial. At first, all I could hear was my own self-destructive voice. During my time on earth I had nurtured these negative forces. After leaving my physical body, the body was dead, but my self-created energy fields were still with me. With Marana's help, I now know that these destructive fields hinder the soul's development."

Guide: "How did Mariana manage to bring you out of your destructiveness and heaviness?"

Natalie: "She let her wonderful vibrations slowly and gradually flow into mine whenever I was a little open. She was very respectful of me and never forced anything on me. That aroused my curiosity. I learned, for example, that all virtues have their own special substance and vibration. One can surround oneself with goodness, with joy, or with stillness, with love, or with wisdom. It was enchanting and encouraging the way Marana changed her appearance. Each virtue radiated a different light and created different sounds. One time she asked me, 'What dress are you wearing? Look at yourself.' The first time I looked at myself, I was horrified at how dark I was, because I was wearing a dress of hatred. That moment of self-recognition began my conversion. From that point on something was awakened in me that I had been repressing for a long time. Marana came and went. Sometimes she was gone for a long time, and my desire to see her again grew."

Guide: "Why didn't you just go with her?"

Natalie: "I couldn't, or at least I was convinced that it wasn't possible. Sometimes Marana said to me, 'My dear, come with me, just come with me. Your invisible wings have grown, lift yourself up, you beautiful butterfly.' But I just couldn't. My new sense organs and my awareness of myself weren't functioning properly yet."

Guide: "Were there other helpers to assist you?"

Natalie: "Yes, but I had eyes only for Marana. I rejected many an outstretched hand. That's how it was on earth. There were also beings that were good to me, but I couldn't be convinced by words; they had the opposite effect. I always wanted to be right."

Guide: "What was the thing you disliked the most in the dark zone?"

Natalie: "Looking back on my past life and recognizing the role I had played in what had happened. I felt the pain that I caused my husband through my stubbornness. Once Marana said to me, 'I miss your presence, little Natalie.' From then on my only wish was to stabilize my inner harmony."

Guide: "Then Marana was like an angel to you?"

Natalie: "The first time I became aware that I didn't have a physical body anymore and saw Marana, I thought she was my guardian angel and I told her so. Marana laughed joyfully and I recognized the color and sound of laughter. Then I laughed with her, my first laugh in a very long time. Immediately, the darkness that I was trapped in lightened. Marana said, "We touch heaven with our laughter and it lets us blossom."'

Guide: "When was the time ripe for Marana to lead you to your soul group?"

Natalie: "Every time Marana came she encouraged me to tear off the veil of heaviness. Then one day, she came to me accompanied by a being of light. I believe it was an angel. At first, I saw only Marana, but behind her was an infinitely brilliant light. I flinched and cried out because the light hurt me. Through Marana's protection I could stand it for a while, but then I sank into unconsciousness. When I finally awoke, I felt that my soul body had changed significantly. It was unusually strong and recuperated. I assumed that a deep healing had taken place. Marana said to me afterward, 'Come, we are going home,' and I knew that that was right."

Guide: "How did your soul group react when you arrived?"

Natalie: "You wouldn't believe what a celebration there was! Everyone cheered and told me how happy they were. I was the lost daughter who had finally returned home. I felt completely welcome — what a miracle. Through this experience I felt, for the first time, the wish to make good again all the misery I had caused others."

Eighteen

Violent Death

When a person dies a violent death and hasn't previously attended to his spiritual development, he arrives unprepared in the soul world and must first learn to cope without a physical body. The finer the vibrations of his astral body, the more easily and gently he will adjust to this new sphere. The sudden, unprepared death through accident, murder, war, natural disaster, or suicide, plus the lack of knowledge about how the soul reacts, result in such souls feeling themselves still very connected to the earth. They can even have significant influence on those who are still alive in their physical bodies, if these people have a similar vibration to the one who has just died. The desperate attempts of these lost souls to communicate with the living, and the pain of not being heard, leads them to sink into dark apathy, which in turn can seep into the etheric body of those on earth. A person who prays and meditates and is open to divine consciousness unconsciously creates a fine high-frequency protective shield. Indecisive people or those who are morally weak can be negatively influenced without realizing it by the continual thought impulses of the lost soul.

In all the regions and spheres of the afterworld there are helping souls, soul guides, angels and friends that rush to help the new arrivals. This help is not always welcomed, a fact to be respected, for it is a spiritual law that the free will of each being be deeply respected. Another law directs that compassion always be the guiding principle.

Unfortunately, the death penalty still exists in many countries. This law is without compassion, immoral, and from the spiritual point of view, senseless, for there is no death. To execute a person, no matter how terrible his deed, is to commit murder. Those living on the physical plane have no idea of the influence that the executed one may later have on his executioner or on those who condemned him to die. When the etheric body and the astral body are suddenly and violently separated from the physical body, the "dead" person at first remains in the earth's sphere. Under certain circumstances he can haunt his judge and executioner with all his negative energy, so that in the end, they cause harm to themselves. Whether or not the executed one does try to cause such harm depends on his moral maturity.

People who are victims of a natural catastrophe are torn from their physical bodies so quickly and unexpectedly that, for a time, they have no idea where they are.

They can temporarily lose their orientation completely if they have not developed their spiritual awareness during their lifetime.

Diary Entry

A woman with a fabulous talent for singing decided to work in the computer business where she would be able to earn a lot more money. She worked in the industry and lived only for her vacations. She died in a tsunami. I was working together with some other soul helpers and had distanced myself a little from my group, when unexpectedly I found myself in a very dark alley in the lower astral level. Everywhere the houses were filled with water. Many "new arrivals" wandered aimlessly. It was a pitiful sight. The woman who was my responsibility was bailing water with a tin can and pouring it onto the street. She did this repeatedly without noticing how useless it was.

Guide: "What are you doing here?"

Woman: "Can't you see that I am trying to empty the water out of the house?" She looked at me, turned away, and ignored me, so that I had to speak to her again.

Guide: "What is your name?"

Woman: "You have no right to be interested in my name! I have been kidnapped and brought to this place. I have no idea where I am."

Guide: *"Who kidnapped you? What is the last thing you remember?"*

Woman: *"The last thing I can remember is water, water, water. Where am I?"*

Guide: *"Now you are here and no longer in your physical body."*

Woman (looking at me annoyed): *"What a stupid thing to say. I can see you and I see myself. I have been kidnapped."*

Guide: *"Come out with me. There are wonderfully beautiful places here. I'll take you there. Come with me."*

The woman followed me hesitantly. Again and again I had to assure and encourage her. Finally I brought her to a healing center where soul helpers received her lovingly. Later she fell into a deep and healing sleep. It took a long time for her to recognize that she was now living in a different sphere.

Diary Entry

Bodo died in the tsunami, and his astral body was still half stuck in his physical body. He kept trying to pull back the cloth covering his physical body.

Bodo: *"Help me! Don't just stand there."*

Guide: *"Bodo, get up. Stand up straight. It's easy. You have enough strength to do it. You are in shock. Come, stand up."*

Bodo: "What a nerve you have not helping me. Get over here!"

Guide: "I don't have the power to help you get up, you have to do it alone. I can only encourage you. A plant opens its buds in the warmth of the sun. Open your consciousness to the rays of love. It's simple — stand up."

Bodo remained silent and made no attempt to get up until he finally fell into a kind of faint. Quite a while later he awoke. He was very stiff and seemed spiritually petrified, a condition that he himself had created through his arrogant, rigid attitude on earth.

No one is perfect, I thought. The only important thing is to try to attain a certain openness during life on earth.

Another soul helper named Gabriele joined me.

Gabriele: "It's very hard to work with souls still affixed to earth, because every bit of spiritual life has been suffocated and it is difficult to warm them up. But in the divine order every soul is cared for and in the end will be awakened."

Guide: "Can those who are still living in their physical bodies do something for him?"

Gabriele: "It is not clear to the people on earth how far-reaching and illuminating every heartfelt prayer is. Prayers and church services and the power of uplifting thoughts and real love are the magical powers that help these earthbound souls find their way to their soul groups. From there they will develop themselves further, always deepening their awareness of their oneness with the divine."

Witness Report

"My mother died of a sudden heart attack without having been ill before. We had her laid out in her coffin at home, so that we could take our leave of her. The whole family, her friends and relatives were grateful that they could do this. A short time after the funeral I had a very unpleasant experience. Shortly before dawn, half asleep, I felt myself lying motionless in bed. I was unable to move, but was able to register everything that happened with full clarity. I saw two 'clouds,' one white and the other dark, sort of gray, moving toward me. They seemed to be fighting. The white one was trying to force the dark one away. I felt threatened somehow, but was unable to move or call out or do anything. I was completely at the mercy of what was going to happen.

"I 'saw' and at the same time felt how the dark cloud crawled up my back and attached itself to my neck. I wanted to defend myself, to scream, but I lay as if paralyzed. Gradually I awoke to full consciousness, and felt as if I had been violated. Something had happened against my will.

"Subsequently, I felt ill in my body — dazed, dizzy, and not myself. Every trivial thing made me cry. In my distress, I asked a dear friend for help. We prayed together, called on Jesus Christ, Mother Mary, all the angels and archangels, and pleaded ardently for help. My friend, who is clairvoyant, looked at my back and neck. She knew immediately what had happened and said, 'Your mother has attached herself to you.' My friend and I continued our prayers and asked my mother to leave and go back into the light. In her mind my friend heard my mother's words: 'But this is my Heike.' When Mother was alive, that was a sentence she always used to say. I was startled, because my friend had no way of knowing that — she had never heard it from either my mother or me.

After some further invocations to the spiritual world asking for help for my mother to find her way into the light, I felt a strong tingling in my whole body, especially going up my spine. I was mentally aware of the cloud leaving my back and neck. In that moment all the dizziness was gone and I once again felt well in body and soul."

—Heike from Braunschweig

Nineteen

Help for Souls Who Are Grounded

Even if souls that have died are in another dimension, the ones with great problems crossing over, for the reasons described above, can receive help from their loved ones left on earth. We who live on earth can intervene with support. Whoever feels inwardly called to do this loving work will themselves experience great blessings.

In all the world's religions there are special prayers, ceremonies, rituals, and visualizations that accompany the just deceased. In Christianity, we are familiar with the litany of intercessions during service, praying the rosary, and celebrating Holy Mass for the welfare of the deceased at the family's request. In some places it is common to make a pilgrimage for the deceased.

Prayer is not about the repetition of pious words in predetermined tones of voice. That helps no one! The words must be filled with life to make them come alive. Love and prayer from deep within the heart form a strong, transformational power that sets free a stream of positive energy that benefits all those who have passed over. There is a visualizing exercise that is particularly helpful for earthbound stray souls. (Visualizing here means to envision a picture.) To better understand the technique, we must be clear that within every human soul's innermost chamber lies deep wisdom of the knowledge of the divine spark.

The ever-present benevolent love persists in everlasting silence, as the origin and end of the soul's innermost being, until the brilliant light of knowledge shines through the clothing that surrounds the soul. The following ceremony bestows an impulse on the earthbound soul to open itself to the light of knowledge. It can be performed alone or in a prayer circle:

1. Collect yourself and try to enter a harmonious state. A very important condition for the success of the ceremony is loving-kindness toward yourself and toward all beings.

2. Say quietly to yourself, or, alternatively, one of the participants in the prayer circle may say aloud, "I bid the divine love to flow through me completely, to fill me entirely, to totally surround me. May peace reign in my heart. May healing be in my heart so that I can send it out to all worlds and dimensions and to all levels of being."

3. Breathe deeply in and out several times, remain sitting quietly, and be still. This can take one or two minutes or more.

4. Feel how the light of the Holy Spirit flows through you, through all levels and dimensions in every facet of your being. Be open and thankful.

5. Call out the name of the deceased: "I am calling you," or "I am calling to you souls who have lost your way or are still bound to earth. I am here, in the name of divine love, in order to help you. Here, where you are, is not the abode foreseen for you. I am here to help you find the way to your true home."

6. With your power of imagination and your loving goodness, visualize a column of light or a street of light. Build an energy field of love that can be felt.

7. Call to the high angels of God to support you in your work.

8. Ask the stray souls to step into the column of light. Encourage them several times.

9. Call on the angels to accompany these souls, so they can find their way home.

10. Pray for the stray souls, and let the words flow from your heart.

11. Say, "Thank you for everything."

12. At the end, recite verse 11 from the 91st Psalm:

> *"God has commanded His angels to protect you on all your journeys."*

Say this three times, or sing the psalm alone or with the group.

You might play Felix Mendelssohn's wonderful composition "For He has bidden his angels."[15] If you would prefer something else, perhaps some piece of music that the deceased loved, feel free to choose whatever your heart tells you to play.

Twenty

Life's Calling

Some of us ask ourselves, "What actually is the goal of my life?" When one is young, one thinks about the answer in terms of work. Then comes a period in which one struggles to find one's true mission in life. This striving to find our true destiny is always in conjunction with wanting to be active in service to others. It is often when one is older and unable to be as active as in one's youth that a person recognizes his life's mission.

One's true calling is to discover the everlasting spring from which it flows. St. John of the Cross said, "We don't know the source, because it doesn't have one." Nonetheless, a part in us knows about the indescribable beauty of this spring whose abundant waters give drink to all humanity.[16] The yearning in you pleads incessantly to find this source. It tells you, "The goal is so near, you need only turn around and find you are already there." Then, when you are ready, you turn around and... you look... what a wonder. A sublime meeting without having to meet. Everlasting love is everything that you are.

In the Western world many people have a mistaken conception of life and therefore also of death. This is because the focus and the most important things in their lives are outer objects — their prestige, their external appearance, and especially their material possessions. Many are closed to reflecting inward on their essential being. Much of the blame for this lies with Christian dogma. For centuries the Church has cultivated fear of Judgment Day and hell's punishments. The central focus of its teachings has far too often been threats: "If you don't behave properly, then you will suffer judgment, punishment, damnation." If sermons about the love of God follow on those of fear and suffering, people turn away in disappointment, unwilling to gaze inward. Then they seek their fulfillment exclusively in external pleasures.

Too many of us have distanced ourselves from a life of goodness and from the broad fulfillment that comes from looking inward. Most people no longer realize that the grace of the divine, or Holy Spirit, is always luminescent within their hearts. We don't see our own essential beauty anymore, because from birth on we are preached to about original sin. Our attention is focused so little on the joy of the resurrection, on the fact that in reality there is no death. "In my Father's house there are many dwellings. If it weren't so, I would have told you. I am going to prepare a place for you." (John 14:2.) Our churches are full of symbols of Christ's suffering. The stations of the church abound with all His holy pain. But where are the artistic works of the joy over the resurrection? Where are the paintings about the Easter message? We very seldom find them where they really should be.

Eternal, limitless love that is God himself has only one wish: that the inner light in everyone burst forth so that the grace of the Holy Spirit can stream into each of us and warm us all. To arrive at an understanding with the eternal means to concern oneself with the holy power of our deepest being, with our souls, in order to experience that God is always present there. He is always ready to come to you, to lift you up, to enfold you, to love you. Unconditional love never forces you, but allows you to be free in all your decisions, never condemning them. It waits patiently to be recognized. When you recognize it, you recognize the love that you yourself are.

> *It was, although I was unknowing,*
> *More than all wisdom revealed.*
> *As I saw myself in the light*
> *In a place never seen before,*
> *I experienced sublime things*
> *But I say and sing no more*
> *What thinking I heard....*
> — St. John of the Cross

A wise old man in Tibet once said to me:

Our individual life in our personal, material form is not the eternal. The eternal, which never changes, that knows neither time nor space, which is formless and forever being, is our soul. It warms us. It fills our heart with indescribable joy. It pulls us into unbelievable rooms of peace and tranquillity. It burns like a fire in our innermost being. It challenges us to dance with it the dance of immortality.

The soul clothes itself in different layers, one of which is our wonderful physical body. It also teaches us to understand that we are not identical to the clothing, our outer appearance, but that we are the soul itself in varying natures.

The soul is deeply grounded in God
And the soul's foundation is only moved
By God alone.

— Meister Eckhart

On that day you shall know
that I am in the Father
And you in me and I in you.
— John 14:20

Twenty-one

The Council of
The Wise Ones

Because so many people know so very little about how life continues after death, either consciously or unconsciously, the transitory nature of our physical bodies is experienced as threatening. Since time immemorial, a deep-seated fear of being judged, made to suffer, and being punished lurks in the hidden chambers of our subconscious, creating formidable anxiety about the hereafter. Perhaps this primal fear is also there because we on earth so seldom meet truly enlightened beings who by living their deep love can convey to us what love really is.

After our physical death and a period of adjusting to the fourth dimension, we do in fact come before a kind of court. This court, however, functions quite differently from what we have been led to believe. We are not punished at all, but rather we pass through a phase of awakening. Our soul guide brings us at the appointed time to a spacious, domed hall to receive the counsel of the wise ones.

(Beings who have isolated themselves and, as lost souls, have remained stuck in the transitional zone do not at first come before this court. This step takes place only when the soul has arrived in its own soul group, its first heavenly home.) In this hall, we meet sublime, great beings who radiate profound justice. Their appearance is one of majestic power — their look gently touching, but nonetheless firm. Waves of light of various colors, softly ringing sounds, and an all-permeating love flows from them.

These exalted beings — embodiments of divine wisdom and cosmic consciousness — understand how to make the soul feel completely welcome upon arrival. All the beings assembled in this circle communicate with each other telepathically. The wise ones know the whole truth in every soul. Nothing needs to be proven, nothing kept secret; every decision that the soul made while on earth, and all the events that it took part in, lie openly exposed. Without accusation or bitterness, without finger-pointing, everything the soul did or did not do to make progress while on earth is discussed quite frankly. It becomes apparent how much compassion for every creature was shown and where forgiveness was practiced, including in regard to oneself.

The council of wise ones wants to explore with the soul whether the physical body it was given enabled it to hear the call of the soul within. Often the soul's gentle call is drowned out by the needs of the body or the earthly wishes and desires of the human being. Was the soul able to fuse together with the physical brain as an equal partner so that a harmonious personality grew out of this union? How did the person deal with the power issue? Was the personality able to help and support others? Did the human being conform to preconceived convictions of others or did it listen to the voice of its own inner soul? Was the soul able to lift all the necessary veils to carry out its message of love? These questions are valid for followers of all the world's religions. For Christians what Jesus taught is still true today:

Jesus said, "Forgive." (Matt. 18:22.)

Jesus said, "Don't judge." (Matt. 7:1.)

Jesus said, "Be a peacemaker." (Matt. 5:9.)

Jesus said, "Be meek." (Matt. 5:5.)

Jesus said, "Have mercy." (Matt. 5:7.)

The council of the wise knows everything about us before we come before it. Even so, during the conference there will be a close and loving analysis of whether, in our actions on earth, we practiced eternally valid wisdom or which circumstances hindered us.

Diary Entry

Guide: "Nada, you are the soul guide in your group. When a newcomer has grown accustomed to his "home" in his soul group, there comes the moment when the council of the wise calls him to look back on his past physical life with them. How is one actually called?"

Nada: "Everything here takes place telepathically. I am the one responsible for accompanying the soul to the council of the wise. It is always very exciting and usually combined with reverent joy."

Guide: "Are there situations in which a soul is afraid or doesn't want to appear before the council?"

Nada: "Yes. That happens when, for example, a life was led without mercy or was full of hatred, slander, and malicious intentions. However, everyone who comes before the council very quickly senses how all fear disappears. The members of the council of the wise surround the newcomer with so much goodwill and love that all fear melts away like ice under the sun. Then comes a very important moment. Often the soul doesn't possess the necessary equilibrium to move within the heavenly ether and see with the eyes of its higher consciousness. The soul is then raised into the consciousness of the council members, and at this moment experiences an awakening into higher knowledge. It feels the grace that allows it to view its own life through the eyes of the council members."

Guide: "Do the wise ones explain beforehand what is going to happen?"

Nada: "Yes. With gentle compassion but great authority, they say something like the following: "We have not come together to punish you, to judge you, or to show our superiority. We want you to see yourself through our eyes. This meeting should be a celebration of acknowledgment for you, as well as a celebration of forgiveness. You may now look impartially at your physical life through the eyes of the love living within you.""

Guide: "What happens next?"

Nada: "The council of the wise is always modest and friendly, so that the feeling never arises that it is vastly superior. This creates an atmosphere of trust, and the soul can once again see its earthly life in the light of wisdom."

Guide: "Isn't it shocking for those who led a life without love?"

Nada: "Yes and no. Yes, because a deep regret surfaces and the wish immediately arises to make up for it all, for example, in a later life. No, because the soul is so incredibly overwhelmed by the presence of love. This love stands outside all conflicting feelings. It is full of devotion and acceptance. The only real solution for the problems that one had on earth is inner reflection and experience. It promotes our inner growth. The soul stays for some time in this state of highest recognition and greatest love before the council."

Guide: "What happens after this, when you return with the newcomer to the soul group?"

Nada: "It is as if the soul being is surrounded by a halo, turned completely inward, and needs some time for stillness. Usually, after the first meeting with the wise ones, a new willingness awakens to learn more and express a deeper love. The vicissitudes of life and the ups and downs of destiny that took place on earth are perceived with a different consciousness. A new sense of dignity arises."

Guide: "The transformation process that takes place through the council is so very different from what people on earth can possibly imagine. What a gift! The holy wise ones transform the human soul through the cleansing fire of their wisdom. They let us arise through their divine love and give us the impulse once again to live in accordance with the original image of God."

Nada: "Yes, that's true."

Each wise one in the council takes the soul forward from wherever it finds itself. We have no idea of how infinitely broad and uplifting wisdom is, how nurturing true love is, and how considerately each soul is treated. When the soul is brought to the council of the wise ones, the hall where the meeting takes place is radiant with light. The council sits in a specific order with the one who leads the telepathic conversation and asks the questions positioned in the middle. The others sit passively to his right and left. The soul whose past life is to be reviewed stands directly before the questioning wise one. The council members' light-filled robes are unusually resplendent, and each is different. Many are tunics of shimmering deep purple or light blue with gold. Some of the wise ones wear radiant white robes bordered with gold. They are transparent with light, yet their presence is so powerful that one instantly senses a deep reverence, aware that their lives belong to a different, higher dimension. Both female and male beings belong to the council, although one feels them to be largely androgynous.

Christians will now assume that it is only Jesus Christ who acts as the chair of the council of the wise ones, but this is not always so. He only appears at a past life review when the soul has already evolved and a radiant Christ-vibration is visible, when the human soul loves Jesus Christ with all his heart and a bond of love between Christ and himself has already been formed. Before the council of the wise, the secret of our second "I" — the "I am" — is unveiled.[17] Not everyone who calls himself a Christian loves Jesus Christ from the depth of his heart. Not everyone who considers himself a Christian has opened his soul for the pure divine. Not everyone who calls himself a Christian allows divine love to flow from his heart, blessing his surroundings.

Life on earth can be a magnificent wakeup call for all of

us; a wakeup call to discover the essential good and holy nature within ourselves and to realize consummate divine love on every level, even within the densest and coarsest level — our earthly sphere. Life is a wakeup call to the knowledge of who we really are in our deepest being: God's children, children of love. Day after day we can pursue the pleasures of the senses or lose ourselves in endless searching. We can do everything to keep our bodies young and perfect. We can strive to live in the most beautiful homes and palaces, to become the greatest scientists and win Nobel Prizes — but the anxiety as we approach death will still terrify us as long as we are not living in the inward light of the pure Christ and godly consciousness, through which all fear and uneasiness dissolves.

The greatest saints and wise ones have lived exemplary lives and taught us that we are all sons and daughters of God. Like them, we can also draw from the eternal spring of peace and joy. When we do this, we see the beauty and perfection of all forms and creatures, and even experience ourselves as timeless, immortal beings whose only wish is to let unconditional love flow into all that has shape and appearance. The real human being is without limits and is one with God. True life knows no death. The pure life of the soul remains untouched by that which passes away. In order for the soul's pure life to fully evolve, it passes through many experiences, including its sojourn in the third dimension, which is life on earth.

Diary Entry

Guide: "Ray, you've just come back from the council of the wise. May I ask you a couple of questions?"

Ray: "Yes. I am still quite dazed. I spent my whole life helping others, and that wasn't even what was remarkable about my earthly life. Something that I always overlooked was highlighted."

Guide: "What work did you do on earth that wasn't given as much recognition by the council as you wanted?"

Ray: "All my life I worked with the Red Cross. I was always first on the spot whenever there was any kind of catastrophe. The council took no notice of this. As I looked through the eyes of the council, I saw that I did this humanitarian work only to get recognition. Yes, I wanted to shine and to be praised, but I always acted as if I were a selfless and helpful person."

Guide: "Were you actually aware of this deep within yourself while you were on earth?"

Ray: "No. I was so convinced that I was a good person that I was very judgmental toward many friends and neighbors when they didn't think like me."

Guide: "Ray, what was the most remarkable thing in your life that the council brought forward?"

Ray: "I was in a store one time, waiting in a long line, and there was a mother with three children behind me. I saw her and something touched me, so I let her go before me. However, that was actually not the significant aspect. It was that I was in a great hurry to get to a business appointment yet still let her go before me. This was so natural for me that I very quickly forgot about it. But that was exactly what was shown to me as extraordinary."

Guide: "Can you tell me what was so unusual about that?"

Ray: "That I gave up my compulsion to do what I wanted and instead followed that quiet voice of my soul."

Guide: "Were there other situations that surprised you once you observed your life through the eyes of the wise ones?"

Ray: "There were a lot. It was always for the fleeting gestures of real compassion that I was praised. It was precisely for those things that I hadn't taken very seriously."

Guide: "Yes, you have forgotten those moments because you didn't boast about them. Ray, I have one more very intimate question and I hope that you will answer it. Feel free to say no."

Ray: "Ask me."

Guide: "While looking at your last life, was there any point where you felt great regret?"

Ray: "Yes. I was very inclined to exclude women from my life because I thought that men were more important, smarter, and to be taken more seriously. I had lots of affairs and often left the women in great pain. Because of my behavior, my development got stuck. Looking through the eyes of the wise ones, I experienced in my soul the pain that I had caused so many women. It was terrible. I wanted to scream. At the same time, however, I felt a surge of infinite love and wished only to make up for it."

Guide: "What chance do you have to make up for it?"

Ray: "My soul guide, Magda, will help me to develop a plan. I need her help and support because, on earth, I was not at all aware of my continual indifference toward women."

Guide: "Did one of the wise ones suggest you develop such a plan?"

Ray: "I felt and heard gently, but insistently, that I should work out such a plan quickly, which I am very willing to do."

Guide: "Might that mean that a new life on earth is envisioned for you, where you will be able to practice making amends?"

Ray: "I don't know yet, but it is probable. At the moment, I still can't get used to thinking like this. Magda and my friends will help me make a plan."

Guide: "Ray, thank you for being so honest and willing to talk about what you experienced with the council of the wise."

Twenty-two

The Soul Self
And the Ego Self

In everyday speech we say "I" and thereby convey a deceptive sense of self-identity referring to our bodies and our minds. This is an enormous error. Imagine yourself standing in front of a mirror: you know that you are not the mirror picture; that picture is only a copy, a reflection of the reality of the person who stands before it. The true "I" that is you is your soul, which wears different clothing. These clothes reflect something of the soul but are not the soul itself. The difference between a dress from the closet and the dress of our physical body is that the body possesses its own intelligence and is an inseparable part of the universal intelligence. Although the body has its own body-intelligence, it cannot differentiate between a real situation and a thought. It reacts exactly the same to thoughts as to outer reality. For example, if you think intensively about a lemon, your mouth will begin to pucker. Usually, it is not about lemons, but the voice in our head talks incessantly from dawn till dusk, telling us stories that the body believes. When the body reacts to these thoughts, then our emotions are aroused.

The ego self, or "ego-I," reflects the accepted but mistaken idea about the self being wholly formed through an equilibrium of mind, body, and emotions. Naturally the degree of identification is different from person to person, but we all know how often the voice of the "ego-I" intervenes to disrupt our lives. If we can recognize this voice as simply the "ego-I," we will have taken a great step forward. If we cannot, then our natural feeling of well-being and the undisturbed unity with our soul gets loudly shouted down. The "ego-I" focuses on outer physical appearance, comparing the alleged beauty or ugliness of one's own body to others. Erotic or physically strong bodies produce either a good or a battered feeling of self-worth. Money and possessions suggest a feeling of superiority. The perception of self is often at extreme odds with reality. For example, I once met a woman who had a very good figure, but was always complaining about how fat she was. Another incredible example was a married couple who told to me with tears in their eyes how poor they were, though the previous month they had inherited 100,000 Euro. When I mentioned that to them, they told me with deep conviction, "We can't touch that money, it's the only thing saving us from abject poverty." This mindset is caused by a warped identity that results from a wrong way of thinking — the basic characteristic of the "ego-I."

If we really want to know our souls, we need only turn to our inner vivacity. The gateway is our heart. Here we can experience something completely new, namely, that in our hearts we are not split into mind–will–emotions–body–spirit. In our hearts we can be one not only with ourselves but also with all creatures and with God. Centered in our hearts, we can hear the gentle voice of our soul. It never discusses nor complains with words such as "That's not true" or "That's so shameless." The soul loves deeply and actively. It doesn't create fear, and, if we give it a chance to expand, we experience real peace and uplifting acceptance.

It may come as quite a surprise when we first realize that our true being knows no unhappiness. That which regularly seeks negativity and accuses others is the ego-self. This ego-self is not true reality, but an illusion, a distortion of reality. Every human being deeply yearns for love's embrace and strives to be recognized for his true soul essence. St. Francis called not only humans but all beings brothers and sisters. He called the animals, the plants, the sun, and the wind sisters and brothers. He recognized in all beings the godly nature behind their outer appearances. The way to peace and salvation is to admit God's mercy into the soul's inner space, so that we humans can awaken to the inner light.

> *Once a person is enlightened*
> *By the light of the Holy Spirit*
> *And life in him is ignited by the divine source,*
> *Then his heart is filled with joy*
> *And pulses within his veins*
> *Until his whole being is filled with it.*
> *Then the soul, awakened to itself, rejoices*
> *Because it is in God.*
> *But only those who have been in this house*
> *Can truly understand.*
> — Jakob Böhme

It is very important that we become conscious of the beauty of our own souls while still young on earth in order to be able to understand and later experience the change from one dimension to the next as something natural and uplifting. What the mind with cold imprecision calls death is for a soul experience in different spheres and dimensions. The soul expresses its love wherever it can, or retreats so that its presence is hardly noticed. When the soul has withdrawn deeply into itself and is apparently nowhere to be found, it is you yourself who have withdrawn. Your innermost being has hidden itself because the vibrations that nourish and enable it to express itself in the body are lacking. However, when you begin again to find joy in the simplest of things like the murmur of the wind or the blossoming of a flower, when the silence within you has no need of the outer din, when, if only for a few moments, you treat others with heartfelt warmth and goodness without expecting anything in return, then the soul, your finest inner essence, reappears. Wherever you experience beauty, heartfelt warmth, or appreciation for the simple things, heaven opens itself in you. Many people, though, pass over these supposedly insignificant qualities in their hasty chase for external objects, recognizing only after death that the seemingly negligible moments in their lives were the most important.

Diary Entry

Guide: "You have just come from the council assembly, Tamrat, and everyone knows that Jesus Christ was present. May I ask you some questions?"

After a pause:

Tamrat: "Yes, I will answer your questions, if I can."

Guide: "What was the council's concern in your conversation?"

Tamrat: "The council wanted to know from me whether I had improved my talents."

Guide: "Don't the members of the council know from the very beginning what your life on earth was like and how you developed yourself?"

Tamrat: "Yes, of course, but everyone must learn to recognize for themselves their own further development. Otherwise there is a danger of slipping back into the same mistakes again."

Guide: "Is there anything that is higher than the council?"

Tamrat: "In the council assembly the presence of God is palpable. It is a radiance, you could almost say a penetrating, pulsing power of love. Now that I think about it, it is an embracing power and wisdom that directs the council. I felt the presence of peace and love. Deep happiness flowed through me. Yes, a Presence that I would call the Father was there."

Guide: "Could you see something of this Presence? Is it a high energy source?"

Tamrat: "No, it is not an energy source that hovers over the council. It is the all-penetrating Principle of Love that is so liberating. It is pure truth, permeating everything."

Guide: "Is this truth God?"

Tamrat: "The kingdom of God is Truth. Jesus, the Son of God, is Truth. Unconditional, absolute love and boundless being is Truth. The super-conscious is Truth. The Truth cannot be altered and is self-illuminating. The word 'God' is *the description of a higher, all-penetrating power of love in which all that is exists. We live in God; in the everlasting source."*

Guide: "What did you become especially aware of at the council meeting?"

Tamrat: "I am going to be trained and promoted to be a soul teacher. I have become deeply aware that most of mankind dies in complete ignorance of their spiritual existence. For every person there are many possibilities available for spiritual evolution. The capacity to experience God's Love increases exponentially when I open myself to love's many aspects. Besides that, it has become very clear to me that to live a Christian life means to resemble Christ. Not everyone who considers himself a Christian is filled with Christ's love."

Guide: "Jesus Christ was present at the council meeting. What was that like for you?"

Tamrat: "It was overwhelming. Actually, I don't want to talk about it. My mind is still dazed from the intensity of the light. At first, I was incapable of reacting, because everything in and around me was devotion and love. It wasn't that Jesus actually said anything. No. His Presence was so radiant that it was as if the light were a blazing ray of fire. It had a power and glow that swooped me up, but at the same time was mild and gentle like the heart of a loving mother. I opened myself in complete devotion and united myself with Him in beholding the immeasurable."

A pause.

Guide: "Why do you think that Jesus was there with you at the council?"

Tamrat: "Because I love Jesus unconditionally. Even while I was alive on earth the light of Christ awakened in me. My most earnest efforts were to align myself with this inner light."

Guide: "Can you explain that a little more clearly, Tamrat? What do you mean by the awakening of Christ's light?"

Tamrat: "The inner light is the frequency of pure, absolute peace and compassion, the seed of which lives in every human heart. When the seed opens and sprouts, a person's whole consciousness changes. This builds the bridge between heaven and earth, or to put it differently, the birth of Christ takes place within, and the person begins to become more like Christ."

Guide: "I would appreciate it if you could give me an example of what this is like from your point of view."

Tamrat: "On earth Jesus Christ has no body; you can be his body. On earth Jesus Christ has only your hands, your feet, your ears, your mouth, your eyes. Allow the Christ Love to flow through all your being and be its body amongst people and on earth."

Guide: "Thank you, Tamrat."

Twenty-three

Raising the Energy Frequency

The material world is not the only reality, but merely the visible, thin, outer layer of the endlessly invisible spiritual universe. All physical objects, including all living forms, are in their essence multidimensional beings, including human beings. Everything we perceive around us exists as an energy continuum in varying densities. The material world is only a tiny aspect of consciousness. The physical density around us appears to us as real and unique because we concentrate our physical senses only on the material world. The day of separation from one's biological body inevitably comes to every human being. Then humans transition to a different vibrational frequency. If one's inner vibrational level doesn't correspond to that of one's new surroundings, one experiences this level of being, and the light that comes to meet us, as blinding and disagreeable. This feeling can be so oppressive that the deceased sinks back to the earth's sphere, where he must live on without a biological body. If the light and the inner frequency do correspond to the higher levels, then the human being experiences the wonder of continuous "fine-tuning" as well as undreamt-of consciousness and expansion into the highest dimensions of cosmic love.

It is easy to develop the resolve to hurt no one, to cause no human being suffering. The following little exercises can be practiced every day so that the soul, when it later passes over the threshold into a new dimension, has the necessary openness and freedom to easily perceive the incredible beauty and lightness of the other world. These exercises are also very useful for our lives while still on earth:

- » Observe your behavior, your words, and your thoughts daily.
- » Nurture only constructive, positive thoughts about others.
- » Study how you emotionally affect others.
- » Consider that exaggerated spiritual ambition and boundless enthusiasm can easily harm others.
- » Don't focus only on your less attractive tendencies; concentrate instead on the right application of your virtues.
- » Practice mindfulness regularly, and learn to listen to your inner soul's voice.

- » Examine your motivation in all that you do.
- » Be still for five minutes every day and seek peace within yourself.
- » Pray and be a blessing for your surroundings.

Twenty-four

Prayers for the Dying

Praying means opening yourself to the eternal.

People who don't pray or pray rarely and without heart often claim that there are more urgent things to do. How wonderful it would be if they were to awaken to the certainty that prayer binds them to God with everlasting love.

This everlasting love nourishes you, heals you, lifts you up, consoles you, and touches you in the deep love of your being. This love permeates and envelops everything. You find it as much in your heart as in the universe, if you only let yourself be touched.

If you live a life away from God, you might think, *I am living quite well without him.* This way of thinking has consequences, however.

> » When you slowly forget the divine in your heart, at some point you will believe that it does not exist.
>
> » If the divine doesn't exist for you, then the seed of

unconditional love in you becomes more and more encapsulated.

Without special grace one cannot feel anything when one prays, because feelings come from the senses and God is behind the senses. Prayer means to open oneself and surrender oneself to something that cannot be felt. How wonderful it would be if you were prepared to pray, since wanting to pray is already praying. Try to be present in love that is God. Try to pray in a moment you have set aside. Be quiet for a time, and then speak from your heart. If you feel you can't do this, use one of the following formulated prayers and try to fill the words with heartfelt love.

Often it happens that one gets distracted while praying. This is not at all unusual. The more you focus on driving the distraction away, the more it will distract you. Keep it in your mind and try to recognize the nature of the distraction, whether it is worries, pain, fears, other negative emotions, or simply trivialities. Bring them to the divine. The depth of your honesty is also prayer, and you will always be met with openness and love.

Don't delay prayer until exceptional circumstances arise. They'll never come. Naturally, one should create the best conditions possible, but don't let yourself be fooled: the divine is ever present in you, even if you don't believe or feel it. It doesn't really matter whether the circumstances are helpful or not. The divine, eternal love, is waiting for you, for the moment when you are fully present. Then pray. Let your body pray, let your heart pray, let your organs and your spirit pray.

There are many forms of prayer, depending on one's culture, age, and temperament.

> *Undervalue no prayer.*
> *All prayers are worthwhile.*
> *No one is shut out*
> *From God's eternal mercy.*

General Prayers

The Lord is my shepherd,
I shall not want.
He maketh me to lie down in green pastures,
He leadeth me beside still waters.
He restoreth my soul.
He leadeth me in paths of righteousness
for his name's sake.
Yea, though I walk through the valley
of the shadow of death,
I will fear no evil,
For thou art with me;
Thy rod and thy staff they comfort me.
Thou preparest a table before me
In the presence of mine enemies:
Thou anointest my head with oil;
My cup runneth over.
Surely goodness and mercy shall follow me
All the days of my life,
And I will dwell in the house of the Lord forever.

— Psalm 23

I will praise the Lord of creation,
The All and One.
O ye heavens, open,
Wind stand still,
Circle of the undying God hear my word,
I praise Him, who calls everything into being,
The Creator of all nature and all things.
Oh, fire of love, that is in me,
Praise Him, the One.
O Life, o Light, to You I lift up my thanks.
Thank you, Father of all light,
Source of all power,
Source of all wisdom,
Source of love.
Your word be praised though my mouth,
For in your being of no illusion there is only now
Ever renewing and transforming.

— (These words are attributed to Hermes.)

~

For He shall give His angels charge over thee,
To keep thee in all thy ways.

— Psalm 91:11

And Jesus said unto them,
I am the bread of life:
He that cometh to me shall never hunger;
And he that believeth on me shall never thirst.
I am the Light of the world:
He that followeth me
Shall not walk in darkness,
But shall have the light of life.

— St. John 6:35 and 8:12

~

I, the fire light of godly wisdom,
I kindle the beauty of the plains,
I bring water to sparkle,
I burn in the sun, in the moon and in the stars.
With wisdom and justice I bring everything to order.
I bejewel the earth.
I am the breeze of the wind,
That nourishes everything green.
I am the rain of the dew,
That lets the grasses laugh
For the joy of living.
I bring forth tears, the scent of the holy works.
I am he who yearns for God.

— Hildegard von Bingen (1098–1179)

Prayers at the Bedside of the Dying

Almighty
Eternally loving presence of Christ,
I open my heart to you.
Enter and embrace me.
I bow before your sublime wisdom.
Make me a flame of love
That not only I,
But the hearts and minds of all
Mankind on this planet
May experience your wonderful wisdom.

— Ulrike Hobbs-Scharner

Christ, bestow your blessing
So that my spirit may unite with yours.
Christ, bestow your blessing
So that like a spring love will flow from me.
Christ, bestow your blessing
So that all confusion in me be resolved.
Christ, bestow your blessing
So that all fear dissolves in you.
Christ, make me one with you.

— Ulrike Hobbs-Scharner

Oh, Jesus Christ, receive me!
My time of death is near.
In my deep devotion I perceive
You deep in my heart.

O show yourself in my consciousness.
You, my haven and my love,
Awaken your light in me
And help me cross over in your arms.

May my spirit find new direction in this awareness.

— Ulrike Hobbs-Scharner

~

Eternal God,
Alpha and Omega,
Beginning and end,
Creation and perfection,
Distraught with pain and insecurity
We wish to render this lovely, dear person [Name]
Into your hands.
Before the suffering becomes unbearable,
Before this loving body becomes further disfigured,
Before this life gives up all humanness
We wish to give it to you.
We believe that he will be secure with you

In joy and light.
We will always be thankful when remembering
All the good that our lives with him held.
Death shall not come
Like a thief in the night.
Death is a servant
That invites your child
to return to you,
Everlasting and merciful God.
Carry [NAME] now on the wings of mercy
Over life's threshold
To a life of fullness and joy with you.
And bless those of us who are left behind.
In the name of the Father, the Son
And the Holy Spirit.
Amen

— From *Deine Guete umsorgt uns,* hg. von Martin Schmeisser, Eschbach, Ostfilden / Eschbach, Germany, 2001.

My Lord and my God,
Take everything from me
That would keep me from you.
My Lord and my God,
Give me everything
That guides me to you.
My Lord and my God,
Take me completely for your own.

— Nikolaus von der Fluee (1417–1487)

Stand By Me

Christ safeguard me.
Christ protect me.
Christ take me to thy kingdom.
Christ give me strength.
Christ heal me.
Christ save me.
Both in life and in death
Stand by me.
Christ bless me.

— Irish prayer for the dying

Eternal, loving God,
Creator in all being,
From your hands I receive this new day
As a gift of your love to me,
Trusting me
To live your divine will.
Your unconditional love
Flows into my heart as golden strength.
So I trust your divine direction
And acknowledge in everything your radiant light.
Let me feel
What you want for me today,
And give me the courage and trust
To follow this inner voice of total love.
Guide me to my destiny,
Through the gift of my being
In radiant love
To serve you and all creation
As your much beloved child,
Held in your eternal protection
Surrounded and protected
By radiant angels.
Direct my consciousness today
Toward my task,
To release and heal everything from past darkness
Through the love in my heart.

Transform me
Through your divine, infinite love
Quietly streaming
Back to my original being
As a sun-like creature,
Aglow and pure, clear and loving,
As a beam of light from your endless sun,
One with all creation.
Amen.

— Ulla Iris Stienle

The Last Day on Death Row
— For Manuel Babbit

God,
You know me in my deepest being.
You gave me deepest doubt and joy.
All my days were in your hands.
You carried me though my years of childhood.
And as I became a man, you were with me.
Jubilant with joy you carried me
Through all the wonderful days
That were so plentiful in my life.
And full of sympathy you carefully carried me
Through the hellish days of doubt and loneliness,
in war and violence.
In the hours of regret your forgiveness grew.

On all the days that you carried me
And were the ground under my feet,
I learned to trust you.
My love grew to this day.
And that is why I dedicate this, my last day, to you,
Full of trust that you will carry me
In these last hours.
I am like a child
That with outstretched arms,

> *Runs into the arms of its mother.*
> *Bless me and love me,*
> *And bless those that I leave behind in pain.*
>
> — From *Deine Guete umsorgt uns*

After Manuel Babbitt, an African American, had spent eighteen years on death row, the state of California executed him on May 4th, 1999. Babbitt was severely mentally ill when in 1980 he murdered an elderly woman. His illness began in the Vietnam War in which he was forced to take part as an eighteen-year-old in the United States Marine Corps. He received treatment for the trauma caused by his time there. The governor did not approve his appeal, and despite many thousands of letters from all over the world requesting a pardon, Manuel's sentence was carried out by lethal injection.

For the Very Ill

I will lift up my eyes unto the hills,
From whence cometh my help.
My help cometh from the Lord,
Which made heaven and earth.
He will not suffer thy foot to be moved:
He that keepeth thee will not slumber.
Behold, he that keepeth Israel
Shall neither slumber nor sleep.
The lord is thy keeper:
The Lord is thy shade upon the right hand.
The sun shall not smite thee by day
Nor the moon by night.
The Lord shall preserve thee from evil:
He shall preserve thy soul.
The Lord shall preserve thy going out
And thy coming in
From this time forth, for evermore.

— Psalm 121:1–8

(All passages from the Bible are from the King James Version of 1611.)

For Coma Patients

Out of the depths have I cried unto thee, O Lord.
Lord, hear my voice:
Let thine ears be attentive to the voice of my supplications.
If thou, Lord, shouldst mark iniquities,
O Lord, who shall stand?
But there is forgiveness with thee,
That thou mayest be feared.
I wait for the Lord, my soul doth wait,
And in his word do I hope.
My soul waiteth for the Lord
More than the night guards wait for the morning.
For in God there is mercy and salvation in abundance.

— Psalm 130:2–7

~

Words in the Night

Go your own way
Faithful while sitting, awake to breathing,
Focused on my stillness and emptiness.
Surrounded by my presence,
Permeated by my love,

Open for me in every person
In animals, plants, and stones,
In everything.
I am there.
I am life.
In everything that is,
Also in you.
Feel me,
Sense me,
Think me,
Do me,
The next step with open eyes!
Go your own way:
Away from despair, open to your happiness,
Touched by love.
Driven by life in limitless forms.

Go your own way.
You are your happiness.
"I" am your happiness.
Go!

— Author unknown

For Those Who Died Early

Now I know, you are there and here,
You were not really taken from us,
Now I know, that you have often come to me
In my inner quiet.

O lighten my heavy senses
You wanderer along new paths,
I look toward you thankfully
As we approach each other always.

And we are friends,
Everywhere there is space for you
And your heart's echo is never lost;
You are born anew in my spirit.

—Claus von der Decken

For Those Who Have Just Died

Greetings for [NAME] on his rebirth

He who hears butterflies laughing,
Will know the taste of clouds.
He will by moonlight unafraid
Discover the dark of night.

He will become a plant, if he wishes,
An animal, a jester, a wise one,
And can within an hour
Travel the entire world.

He knows, that he knows nothing,
Like the others who know nothing,
Only he knows what the others
And he still have to learn.

For he who yearns within for foreign shores,
And has the courage to reach for them,
Will increasingly not be deterred
For fear of discovering himself.

From below to the summit,
Looking up toward himself,
He calmly confronts the challenges
From his own underworld.

He who hears butterflies laughing,
Will know the taste of clouds.
He will by moonlight unafraid
Discover the dark of night.

He who lives at peace with himself,
Will also die in peace,
And is even then more alive
Than all his successors.

—Carlos Karges (1951–2002),
Member of the music group Novalis

≈

In Cases of Suicide

Unexpectedly we stand before the body of [NAME]
We sensed so little of his despair
And did not register his agony.

We are shocked and full of grief,
And we ask [NAME] for forgiveness
That we didn't see his pain.

Lord, our God, we stand here
And pray for [NAME]
Who yearned so much for love and respect.

*Carry him in your hands.
Be there for him,
So that he may find the recognition and comfort,
That he so sorely missed.*

*Heavenly Father, we must also
Seek help for ourselves,
Because we cannot cope with this loss alone,
Regret cries out in us, and our feelings of love
Now want to flow to him.*

*Embrace us and him in the mantle
Of your great mercy,
Give us peace beyond death.
In the name of the Father, the
Son, and the Holy Spirit.*

— From *Deine Guete umsorgt uns*

The Good Shepherd lead me
Where thou art transformed
That thou mayest breathe
The air of eternal Being.

Where thou workest as soul
For worlds to come
The grace of the Spirit
Unite us with Thee.

— Adam Bittleston

At the Gravesite

Did I ever tell you
That you were a blessing in my life?
Have I thanked you enough
For the lighted path that you showed me
In the barren landscape of my childhood?

You gave me my pet names,
That warm me till this today.
I was always welcome
In the house where your soul lived.

I can yet hear your joyous laughter.
It still does me good.
But the greatest gift
That you have left me
Is the quiet dignity with which
You bore your agonies.
That a person can do this:
In death's shadow to be so simply giving.

Not that nature made you strong.
You were one who loves.
From that alone grew all your strength.
You were blessed and unaware.
I thank you,
For being with us.

— Antje Sabine Naegeli

(Text changed from the third person to the second)

Prayers for Blessing and Protection

Rampart of crystal
Everywhere
Close around me
Enclose me within the Being
Overpower me
Remake me
Let nothing permeate
Except (God's) light alone.

— Rudolf Steiner (1861–1925)

~

May the Lord bless and protect you.
May the Lord let His countenance shine on you
And bless you with His grace.
May the Lord turn His countenance upon you
And grant you healing.

— From the Book of Numbers 6:24–26

Wonderfully protected by good powers,
We hope for consolation whatever comes.
God is with us in the evening and the morning
And certainly with every new day.

—Dietrich Bonhoffer (1906–1945)

~

May God Accompany You

May God bless you,
The Father,
Who created you in his own image.
May God bless you,
The Son,
Who through his suffering and death
Redeemed you.
May God bless you,
The Holy Spirit,
Who called you to life
And blessed you.

May God, the Father and the Son
And the Holy Spirit,
Guide you through the darkness of death.

May He be merciful at the judgment
And grant you peace and eternal life.

Thus speaks the Lord:
Do not be afraid,
For I have redeemed you.
I have called you by name,
You are mine
Blessed in death.

— From *Deine Guete umsorgt uns*

～

May an angel go before you
And show you the way,
So that you find fulfillment.
Step by step.

May an angel stand behind you,
In order to strengthen your back
That you may stand erect
And live a life of truth.

May an angel accompany you
On your right and on your left.

May an angel stand beneath you,
To carry you

When you no more experience
Firm earth beneath you.

May an angel be within you
To dry you tears
And keep your heart filled
With the light of faith.

May an angel be above you,
To protect you
As you cross the threshold
Into another reality.

— Author unknown.

Dying is Beauty

You will always be happy.
Nothing can keep this from you.
You go and beauty is before you.
You go and beauty is behind you.
You go and beauty is above you.
You go and beauty is below you.
Beauty surrounds you wherever you go.
Your words are also beautiful.

— North American Navajo Prayer

Notes and Bibliography

1. George G. Ritchie, Elizabeth Sherrill, *Return From Tomorrow*, from the German (Francke Buchhandlung, Marburg 2007).
2. Stefan von Jankovich, *I Was Clinically Dead — My Most Beautiful Experience*, from the German (Drei Eichen Verlag, Munich 1984).
3. William Buhlmann, *Out of Body: Astral Travels, Man's Final Adventure* (Ansata Verlag, Munich, 2003).
4. Often-used terms in Spanish and German mysticism.
5. Raymond Moody, *Life after Life: The Investigation of a Phenomenon - Survival of Bodily Death* (Rowohlt Verlag, Reinbeck 2001).
6. Jankovich, *I Was Clinically Dead*.
7. See Sogyal Rinpoche, *The Tibetan Book of Living and Dying. A Key to Deeper Understanding of Life and Death* (O.W. Garth at Scherz, Frankfurt/Main, 2003).
8. Elisabeth Kübler-Ross, *On Death and Dying* ("Interviews mit Sterbenden") from the German (Verlag Droemer Knaur, Munich 2001).

9. Daniela Tausch-Flammer, "On One's Deathbed Time Is Most Precious," article in Public Forum Extra: "Dying with Dignity," August 2005.
10. funeral network e.V. — a nonprofit organization for dying and funeral culture, Wohnstr. 20, 34123 Kassel, Germany. Web: www.sterbekultur.de, March 2007.
11. Frederick Lenz, *Lifetimes. True Accounts of Reincarnation* (New York: The Bobbs-Merrill Company, 1979).
12. Jankovich, *I Was Clinically Dead*.
13. Flavio M. Cabobianco, *I Come from the Sun* (Ch. Falk Verlag, Seeon 2004).
14. An interesting page about alternative burials with additional links may be found at http://postmortal.de/Bestattung-Beisetzung/Alternativen/alternativen.html (March 2007).
15. Kirchenwerk V, Kammerchor Stuttgart, Frieder Bernius, Carus-Verlag, Stuttgart, Nr. 83.203.
16. St. John of the Cross, *Singers of Love* (Echter Verlag, Würzburg, Germany, 1985).
17. See Ulrike Hobbs-Scharner, *The Interior Castle* (HMHE-Verlag, Vogtsburg, Germany, 2004).